Totems in and near Ketchikan Alaska

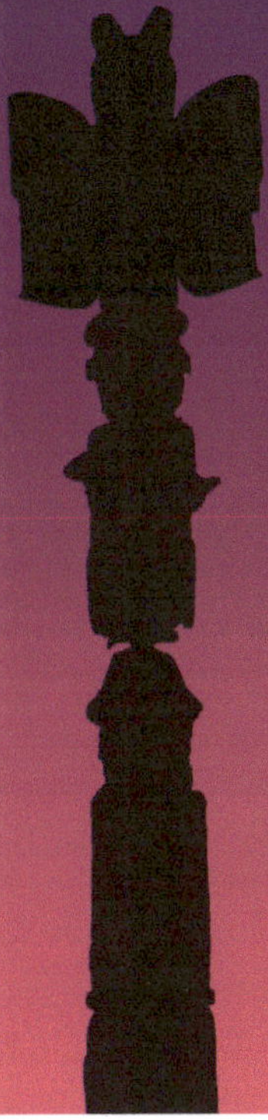

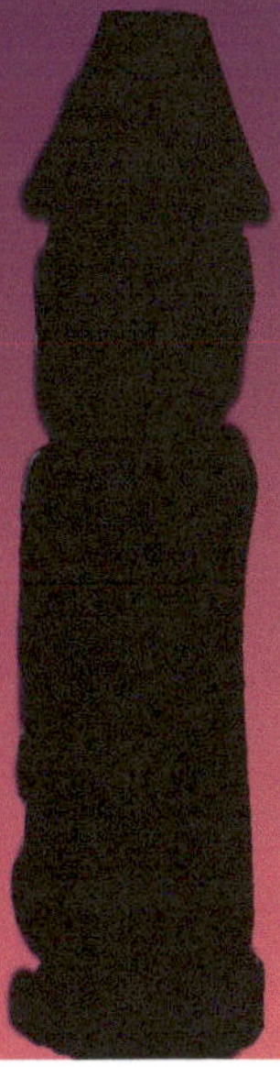

2019
Sp8s Studio

Totem poles tell stories.
Totem poles display history.
Totem pole stories are past down.
There are many totem poles,
many are found in Alaska.
Ketchikan has one of the largest
collections, and it is still being added to.
Totem pole carvers are rare and special.
This E-Book displays many of the totem
poles that are found in and near
Ketchikan Alaska, which is in the SE part
of Alaska. Some of the pictures only show
the totems in color with a blurry background. .
While others display totems as they are seen.
We hope you enjoy this book. This book does
not display all of the totems found here.

If any of the totems were misnamed,
or if there are errors we're sorry and
we were not trying to provide
false or incorrect information. We tried
to double check the names before this
was published. The ones that are in black type,
are the ones we were unable to find the name
or unsure of the correct name. Please drop
us an email with any corrections,
Information or any praises at
sp8s-studio@outlook.com. Thank you
for purchasing this E-Book. For info
on our other E-Books published, or info
on Alaska or some of our travels, please
See our site at:
www.sp8sstudio.com

Cape Fox Totems

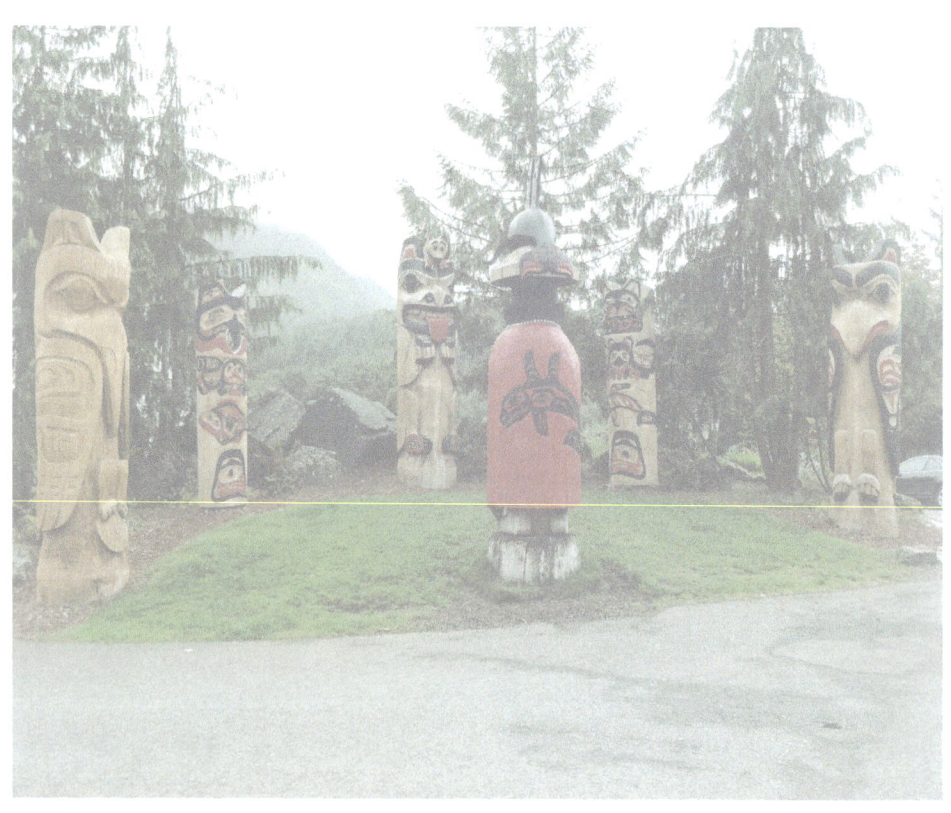

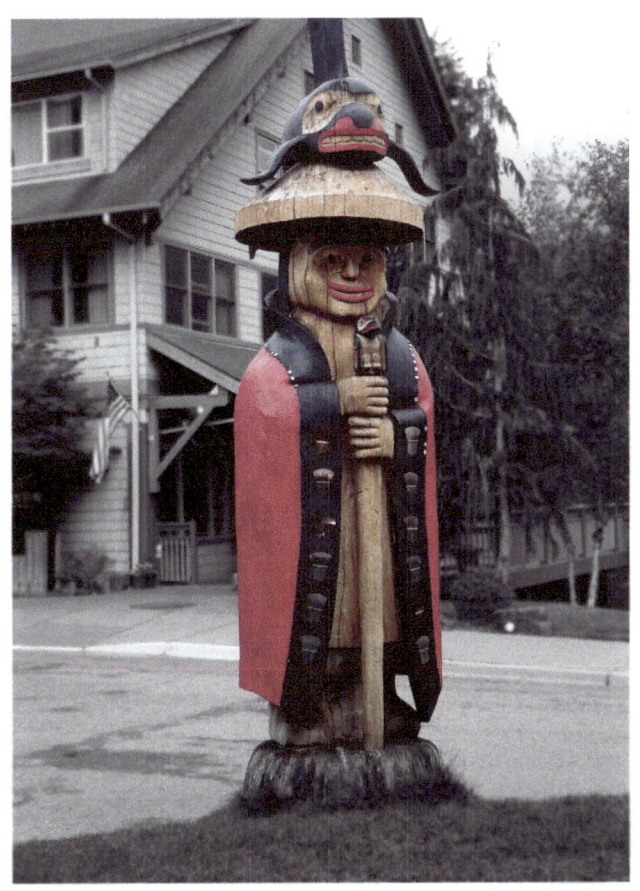

The Naa Kaani Pole

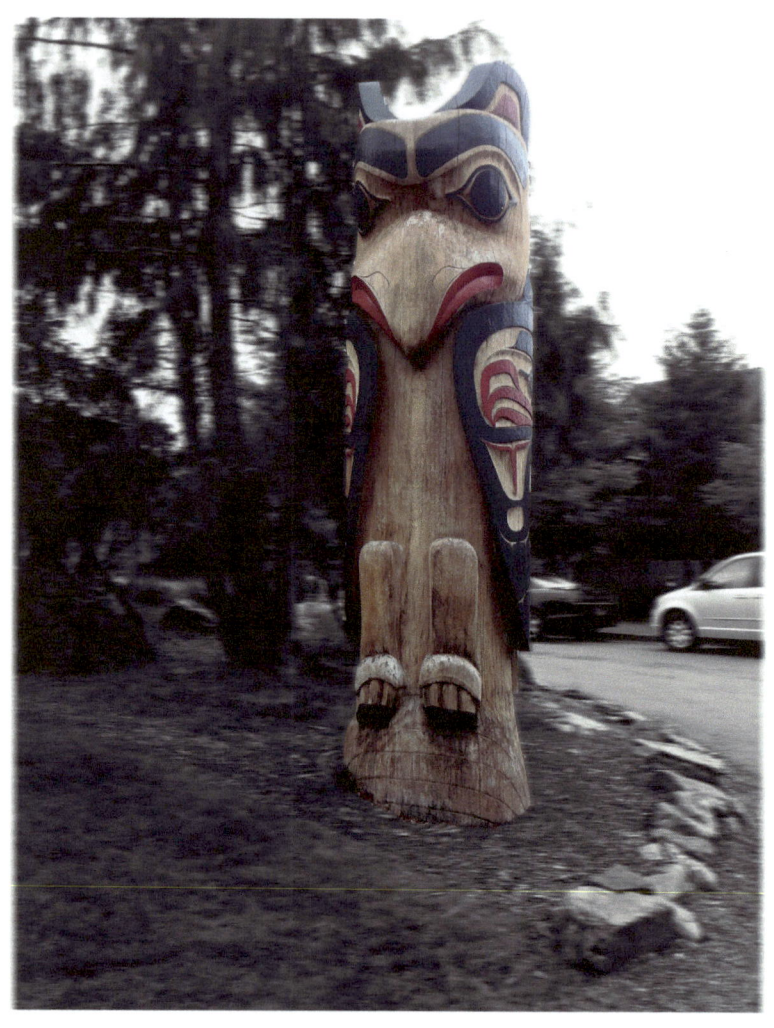

???

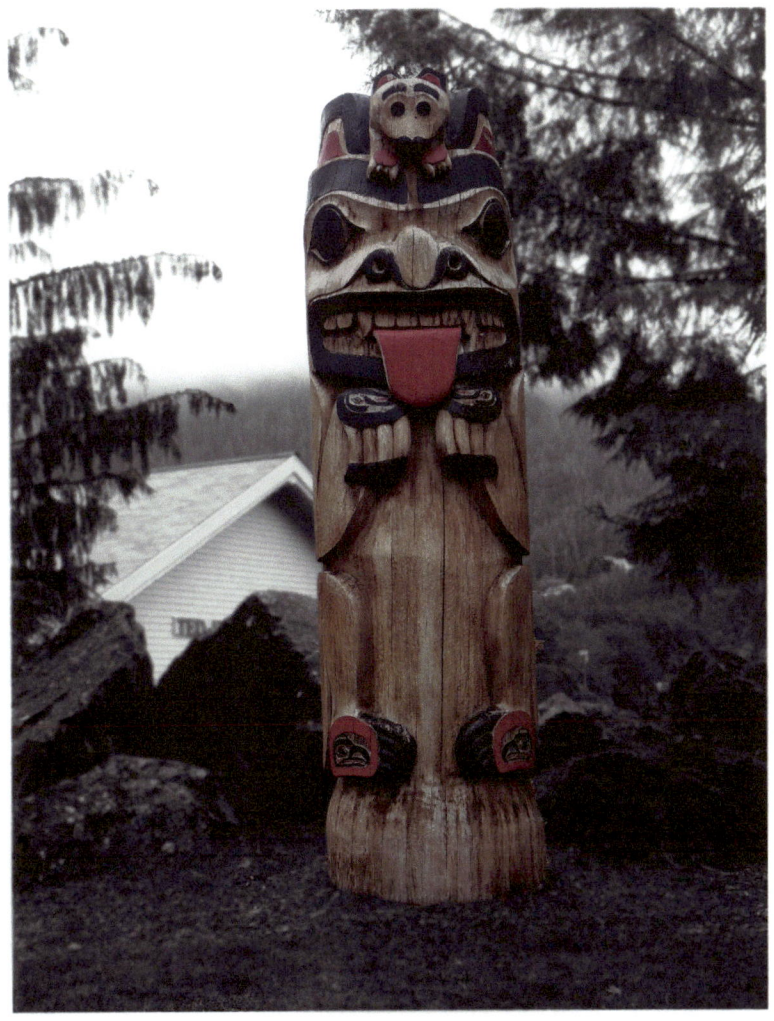

The Brown Bear Pole

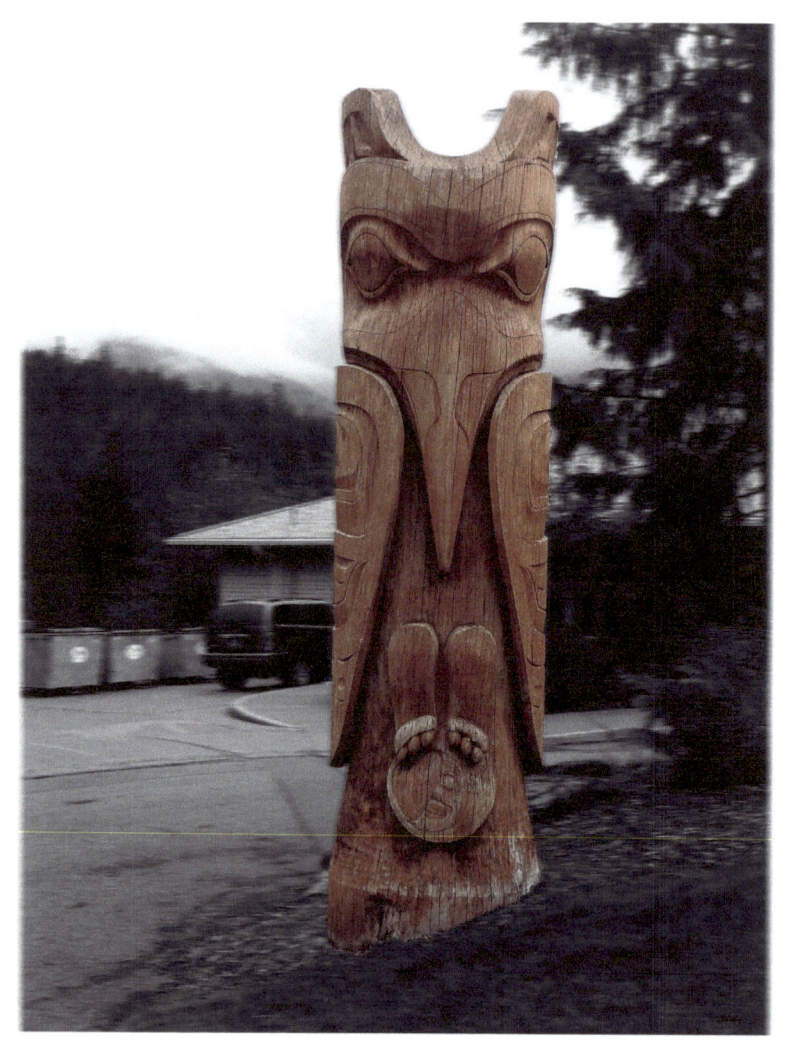

???

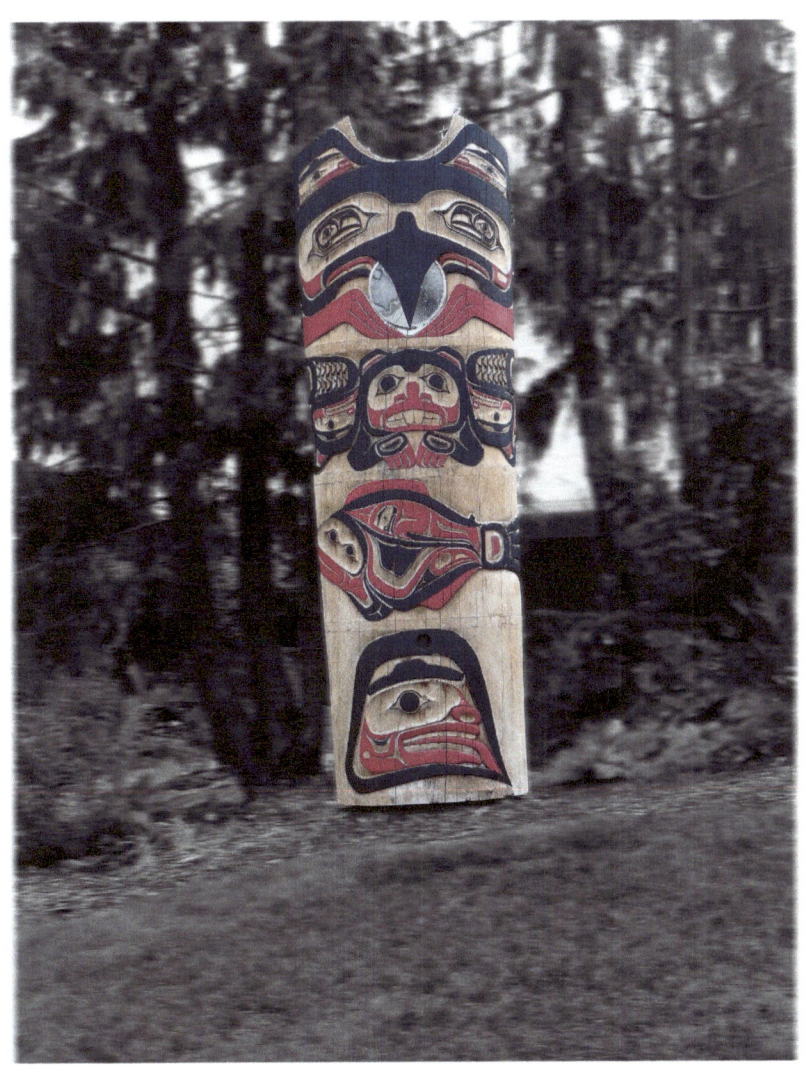

Raven Stealing the Moon and Stars Pole

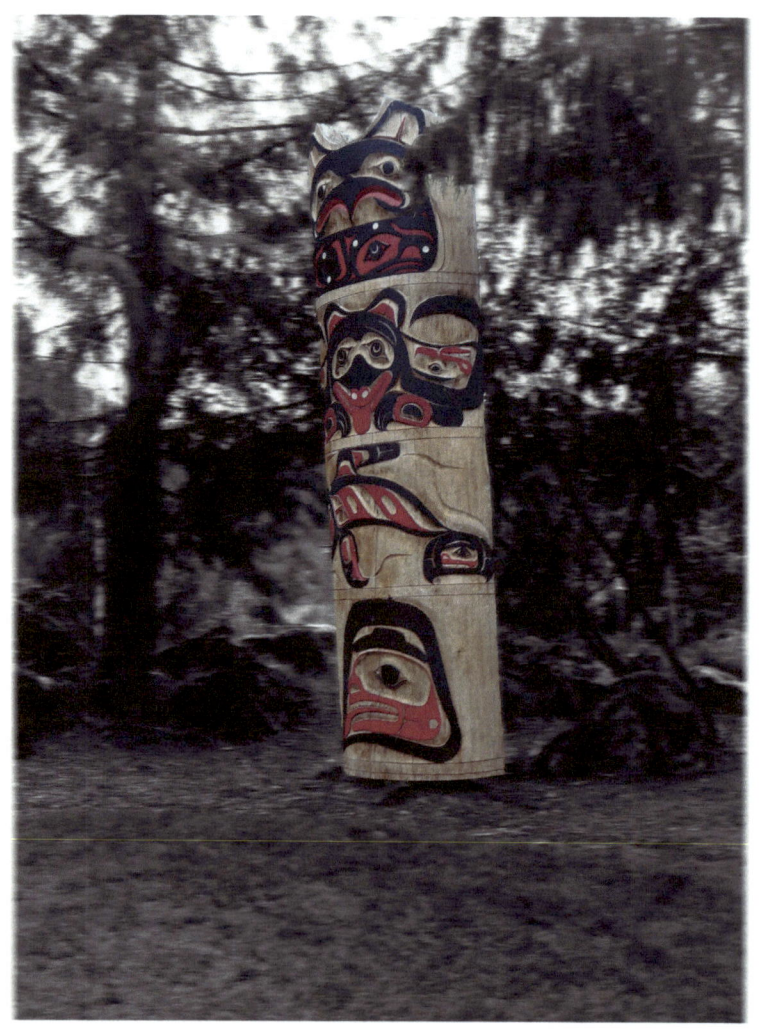

???

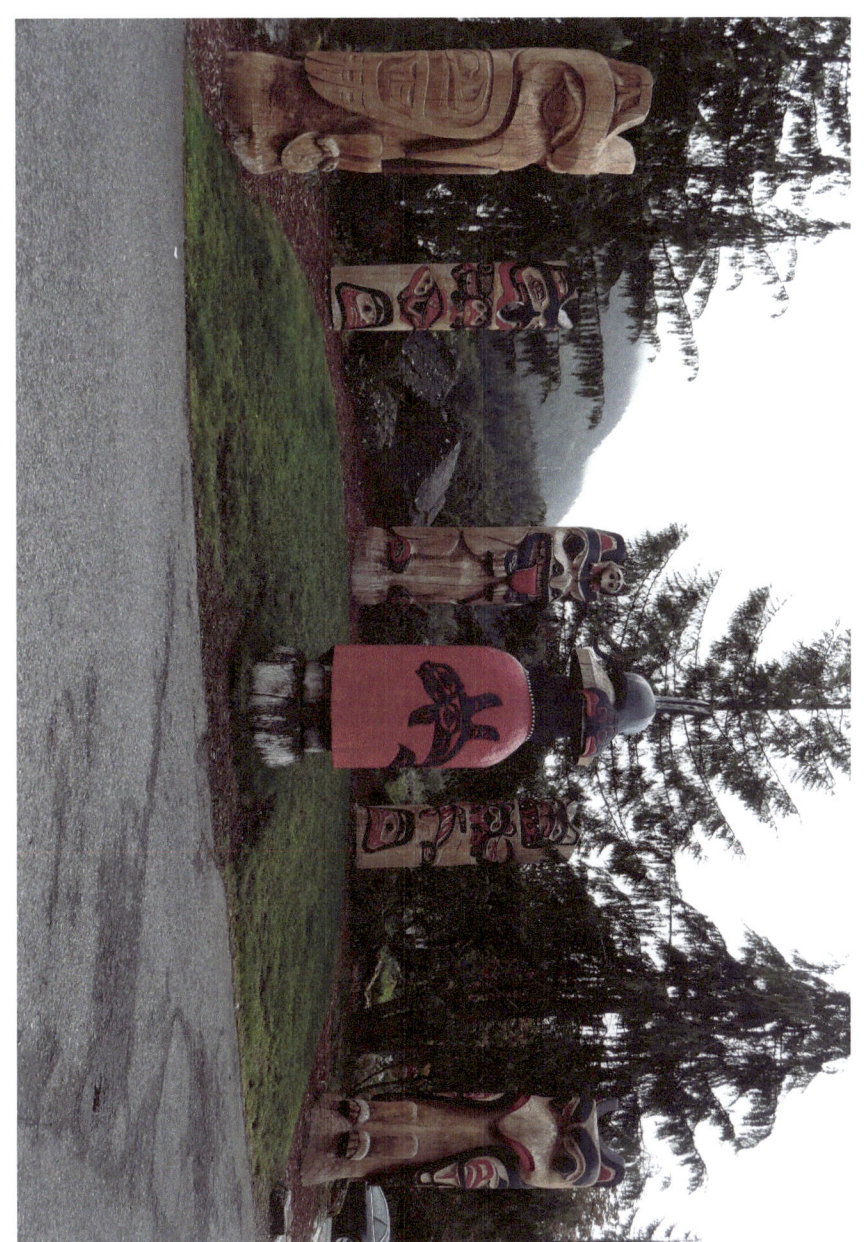

Council of the Clans (Totem Circle)

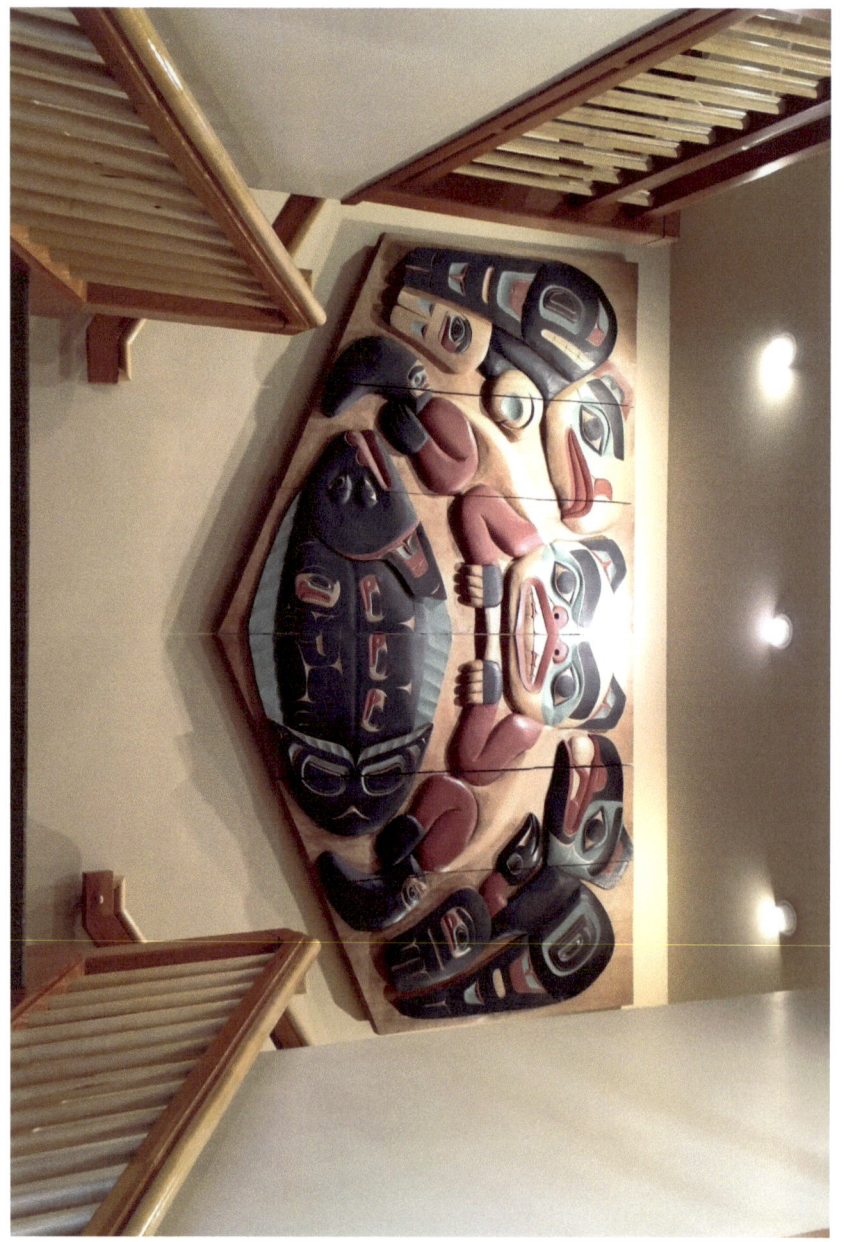

Inside Cape Fox

Totem Bight State Park and Potlatch Park

9883 N Tongass Highway
Bight = bay, Totm Bight = Bay with totems
33 acres
Built in 1940
Admission $ 5.00 for Totem Bight park,
Potlatch park is right next to Totem Bight.

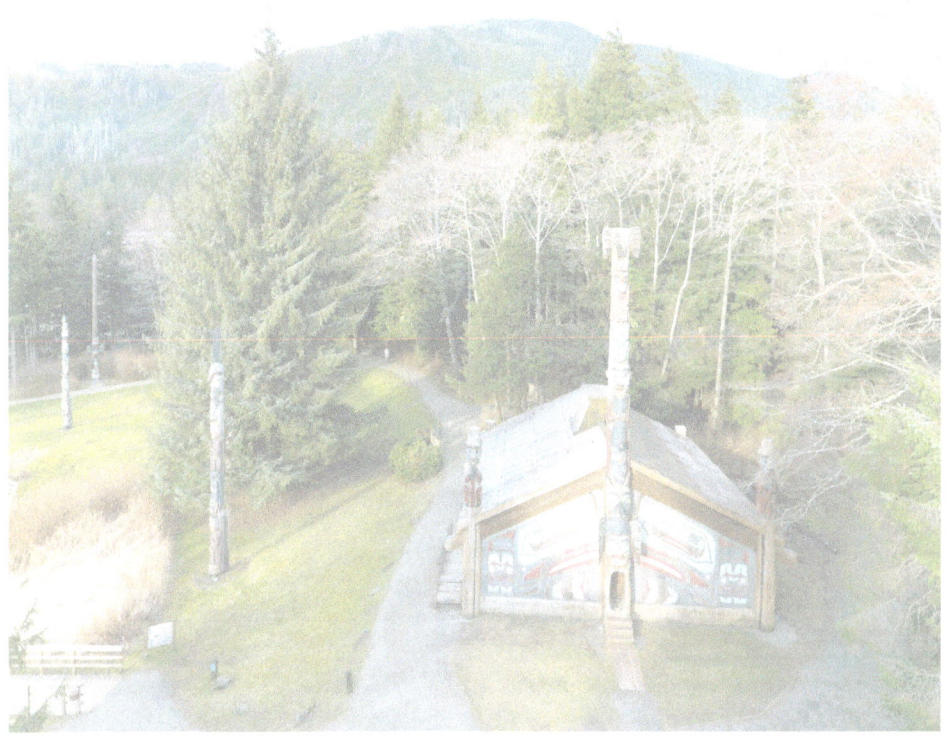

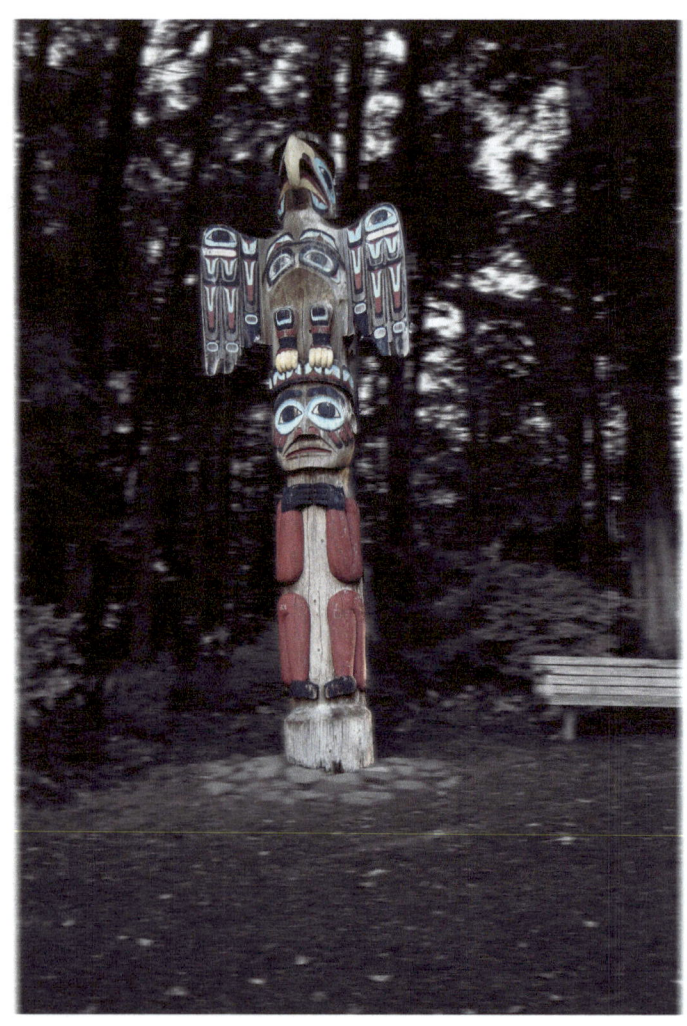

Eagle Grave Marker Pole

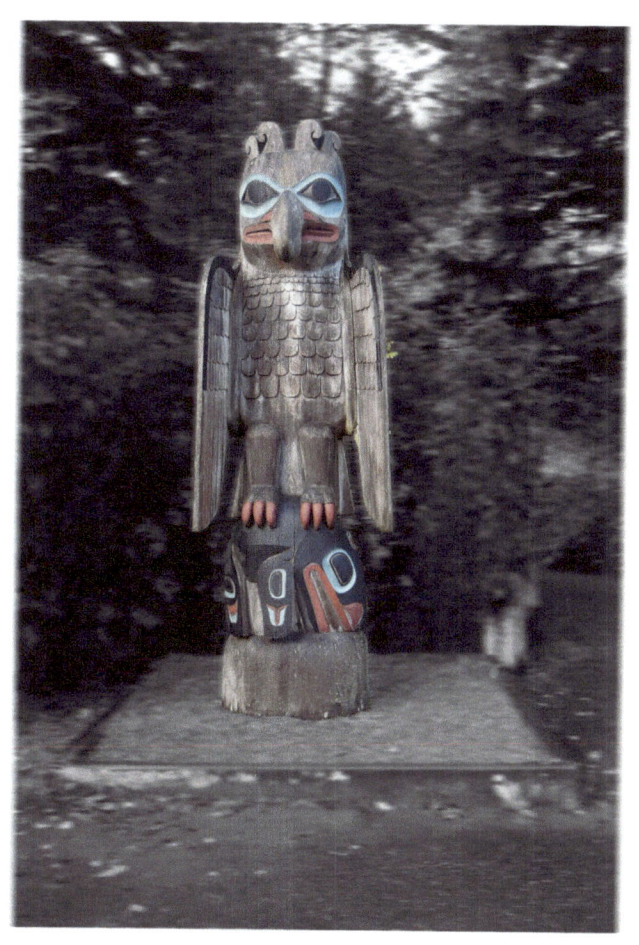

Thunderbird Whale Mortuary Pole

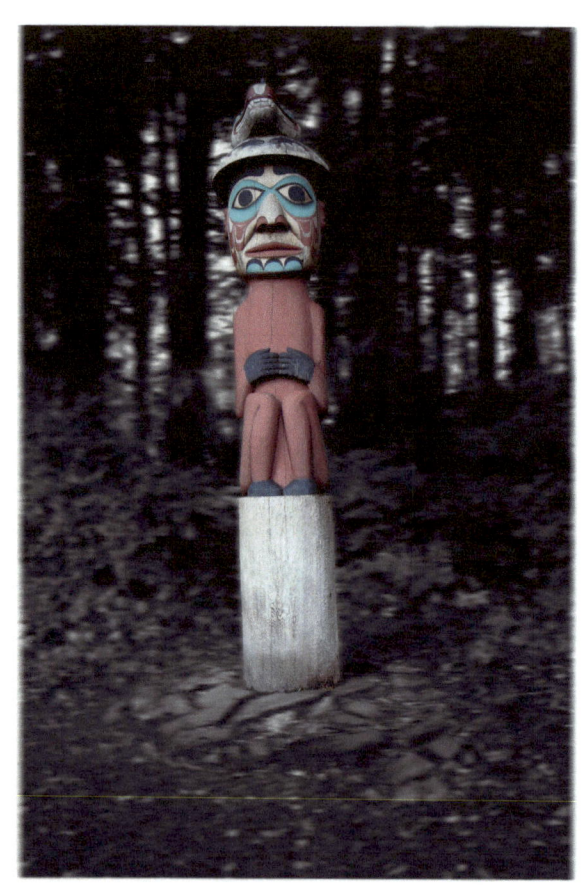

Man wearing Bear Hat Pole

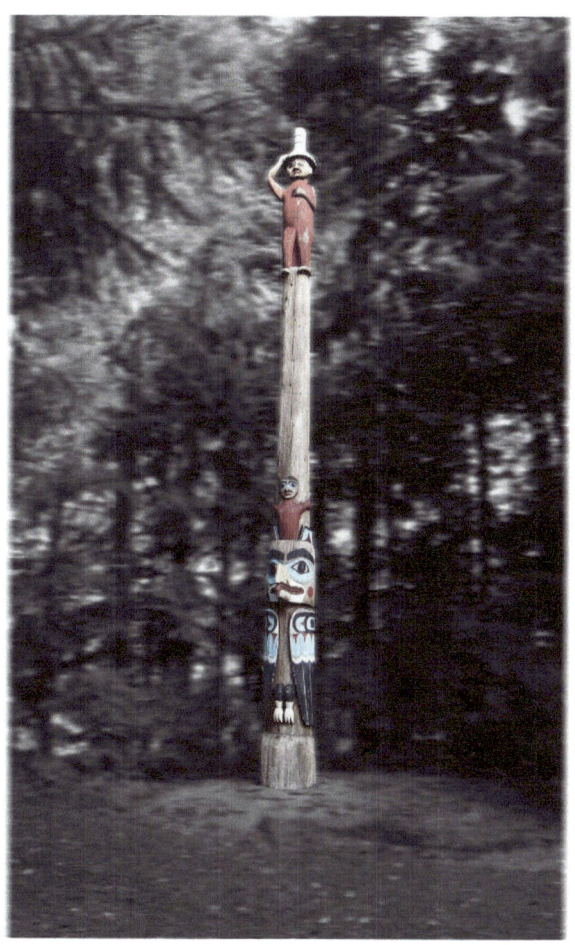

Sea Monster Pole ?

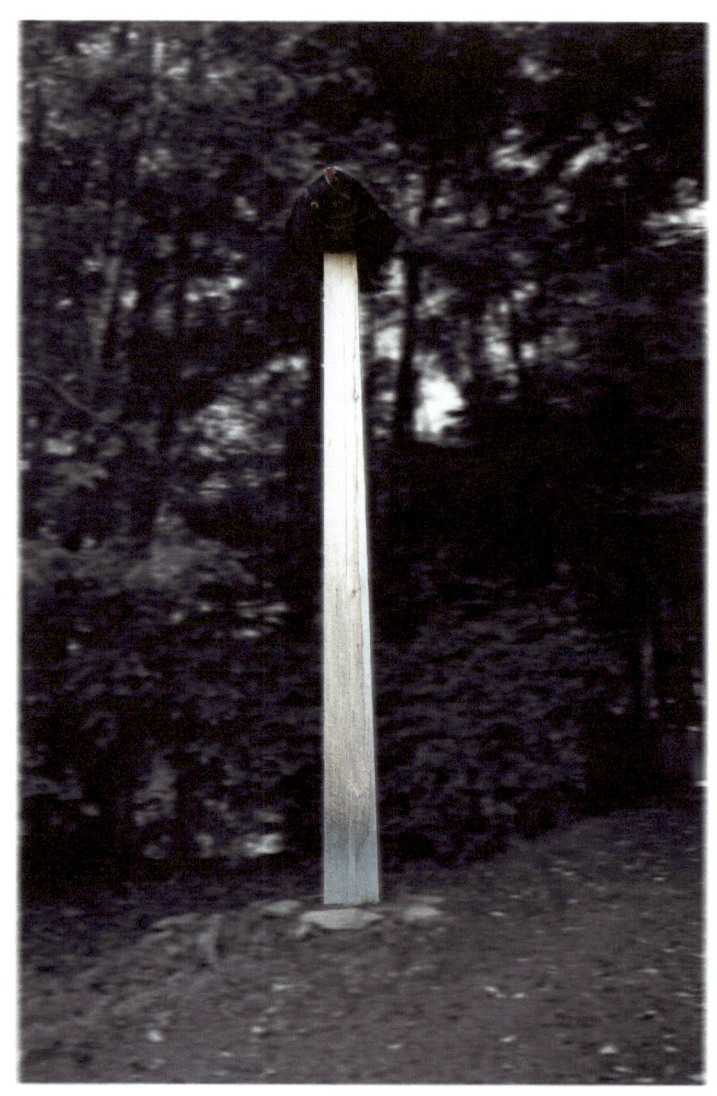

Halibut Pole

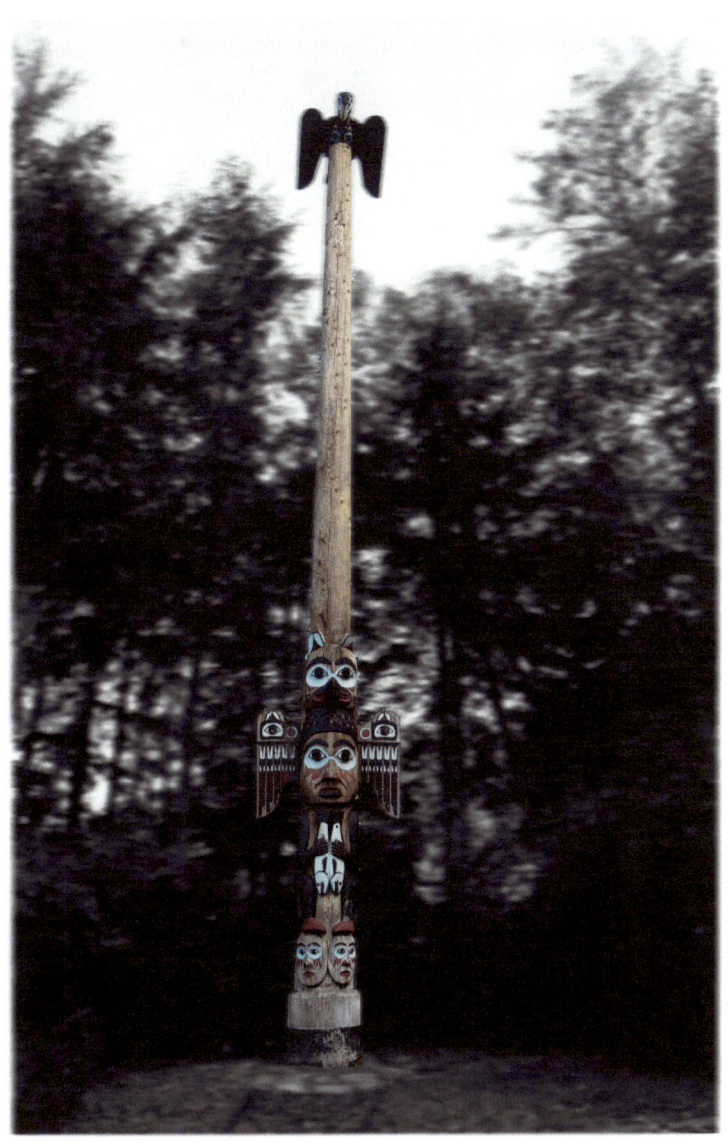

Kadjuk Bird Pole

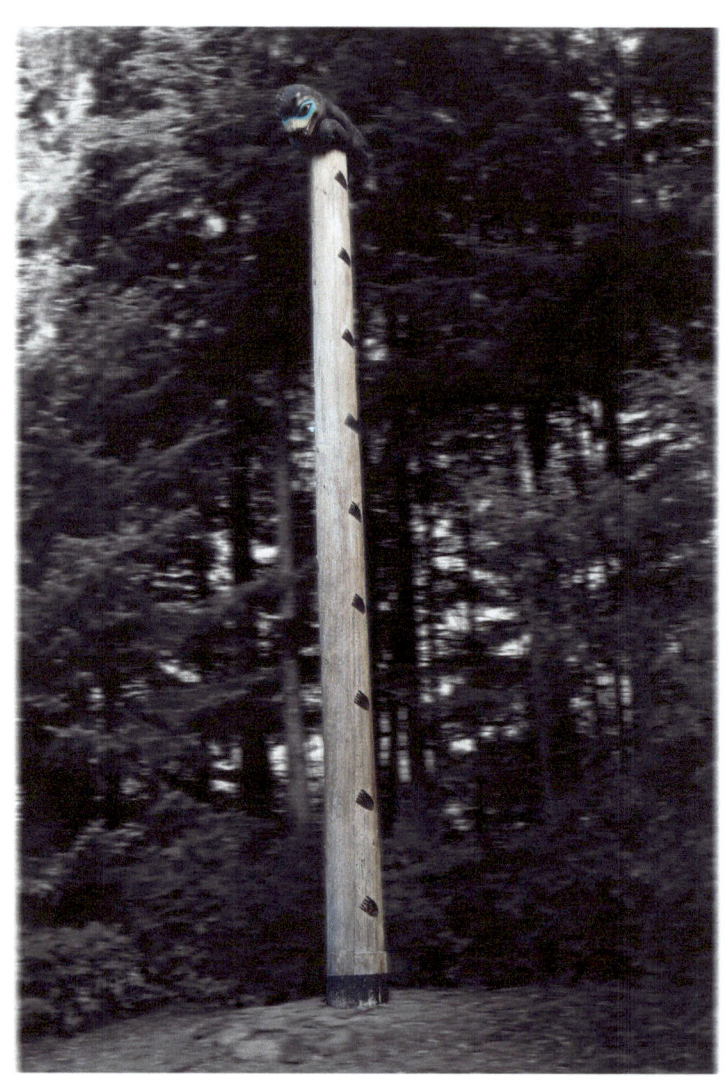

Katz Bear Wife Pole

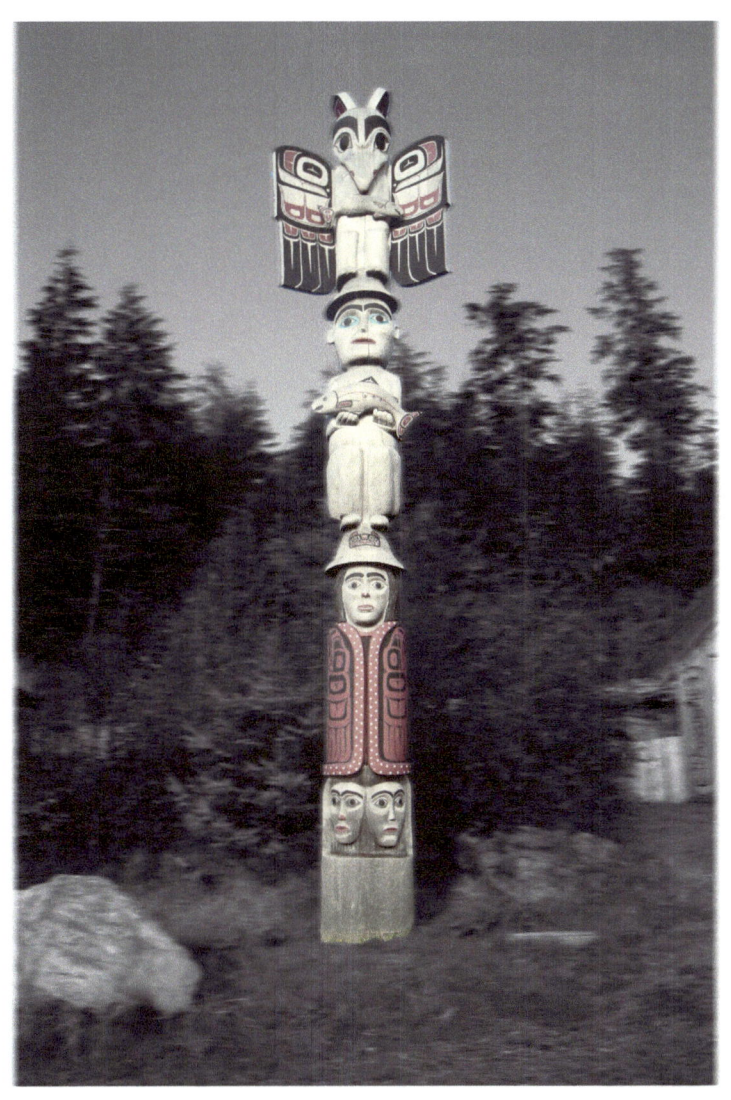
???

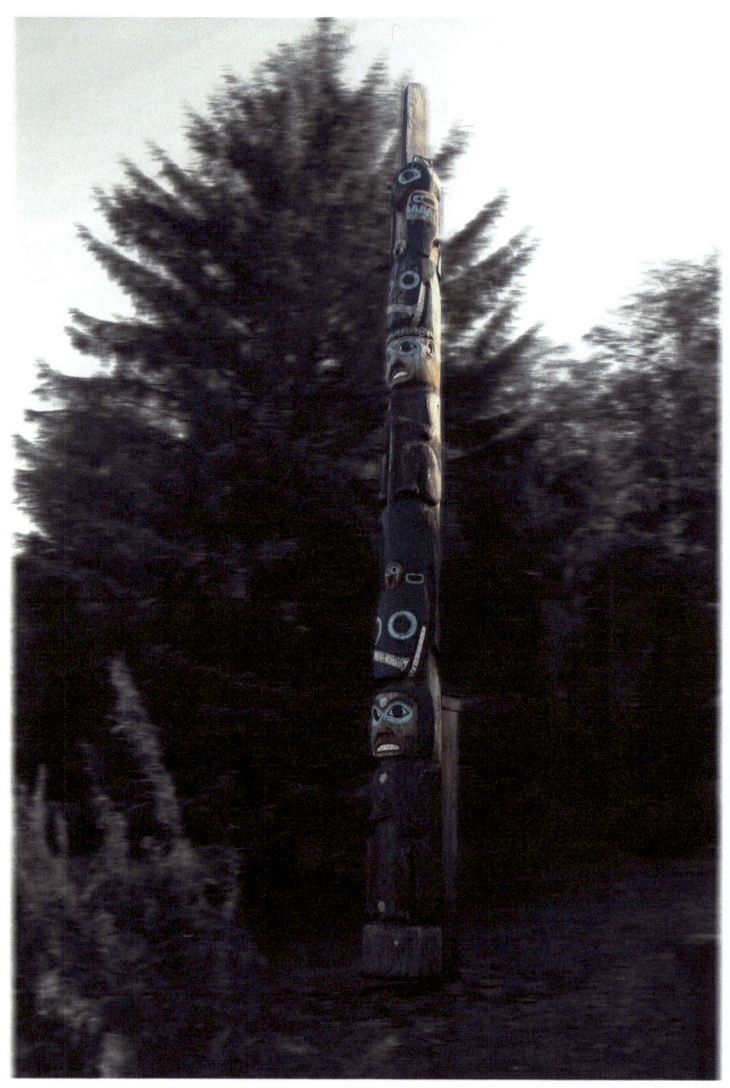

Blackfish Pole

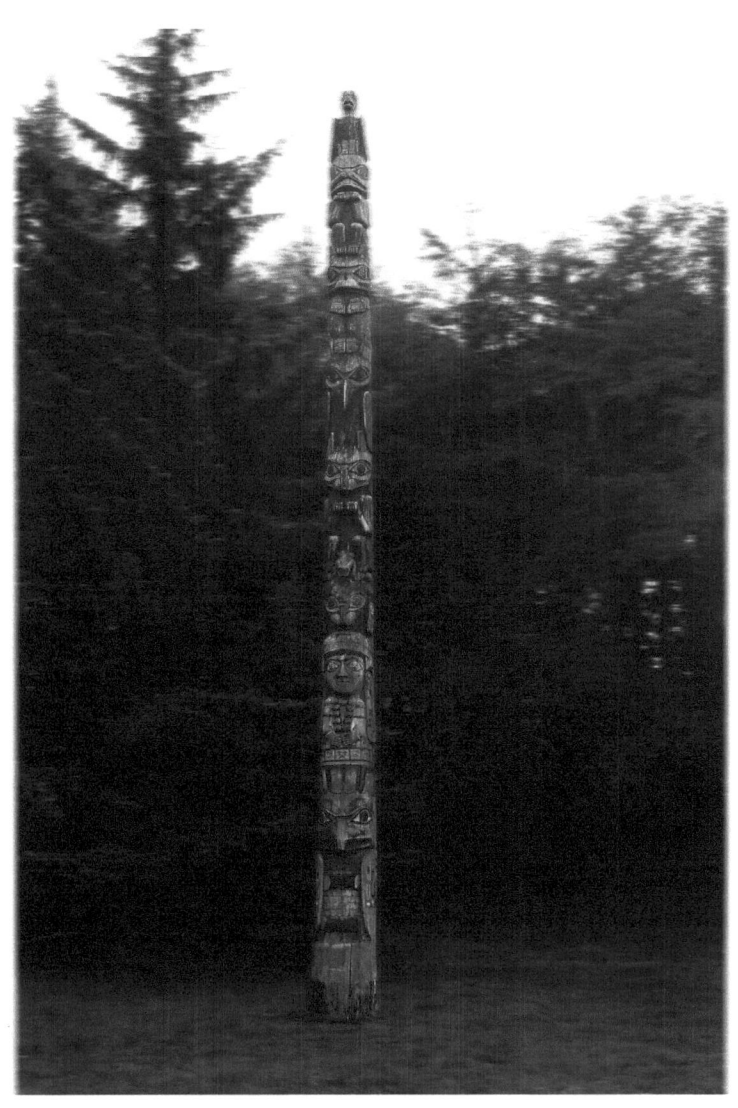

Master Carver Pole ?

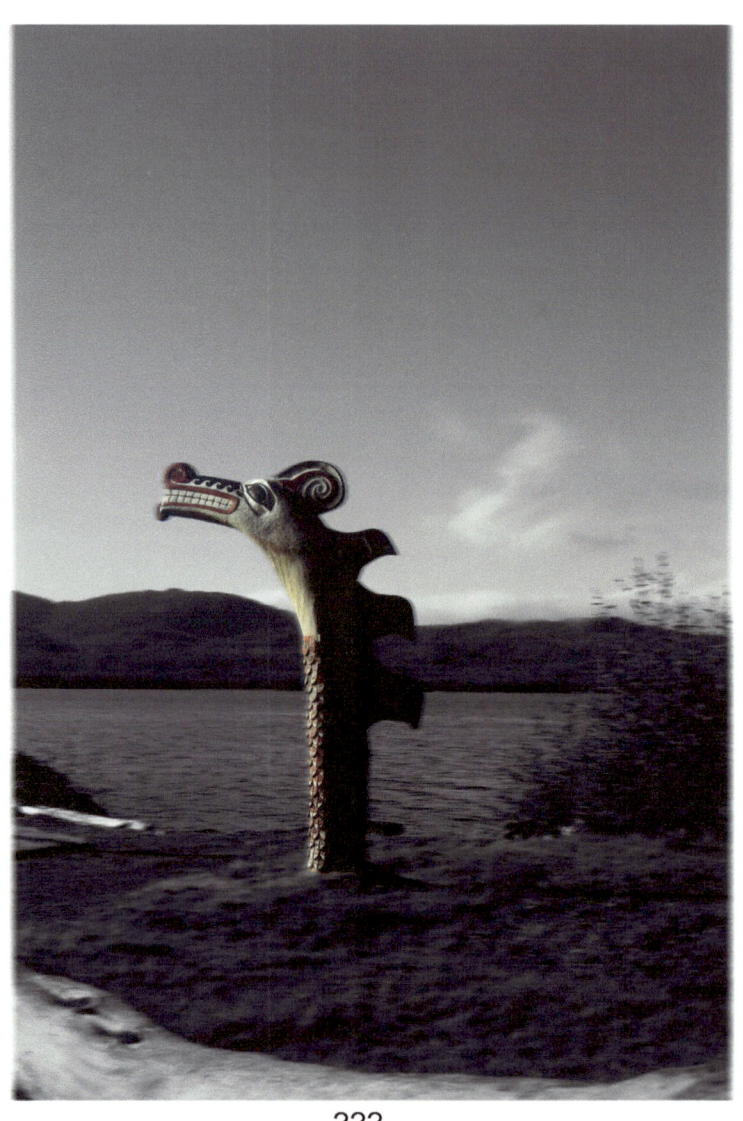

???

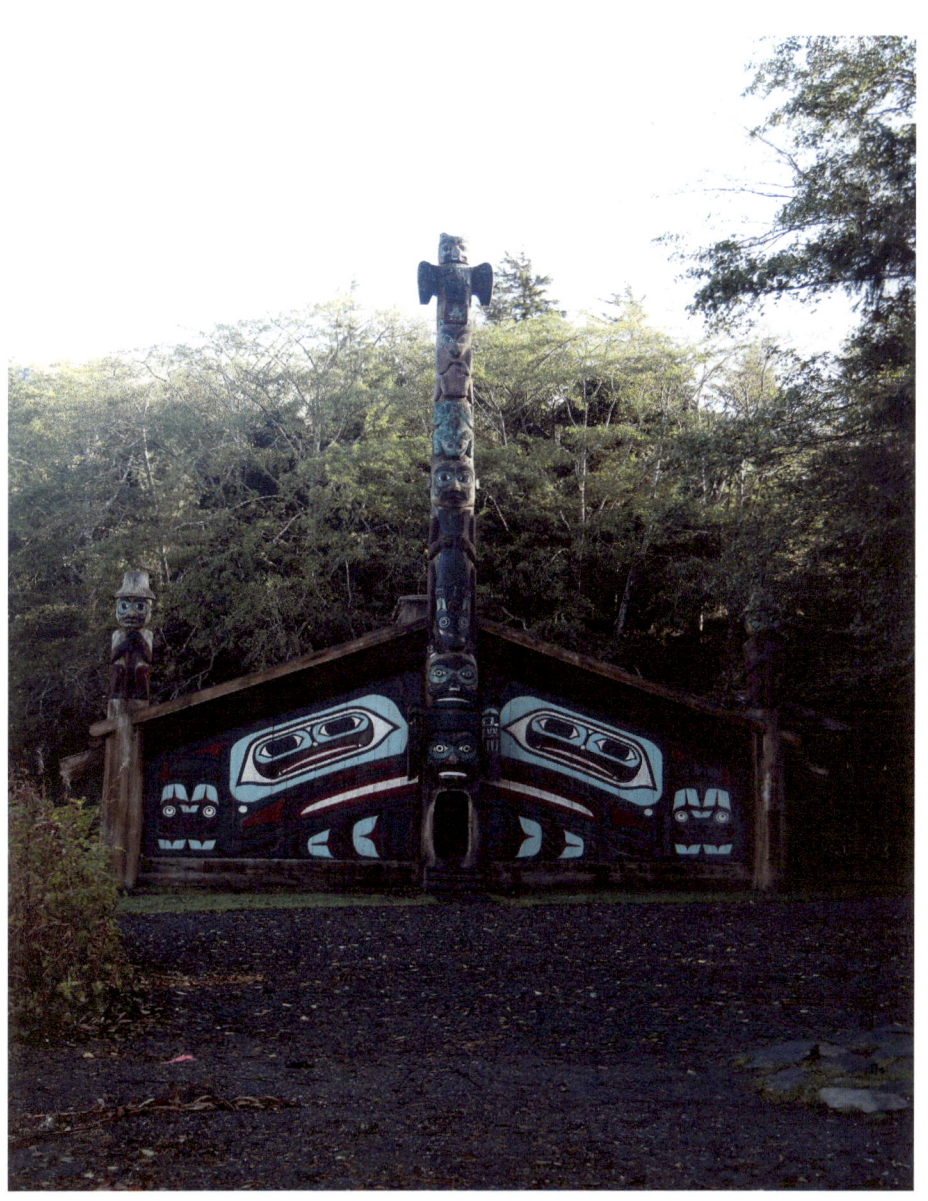

The Clanhouse

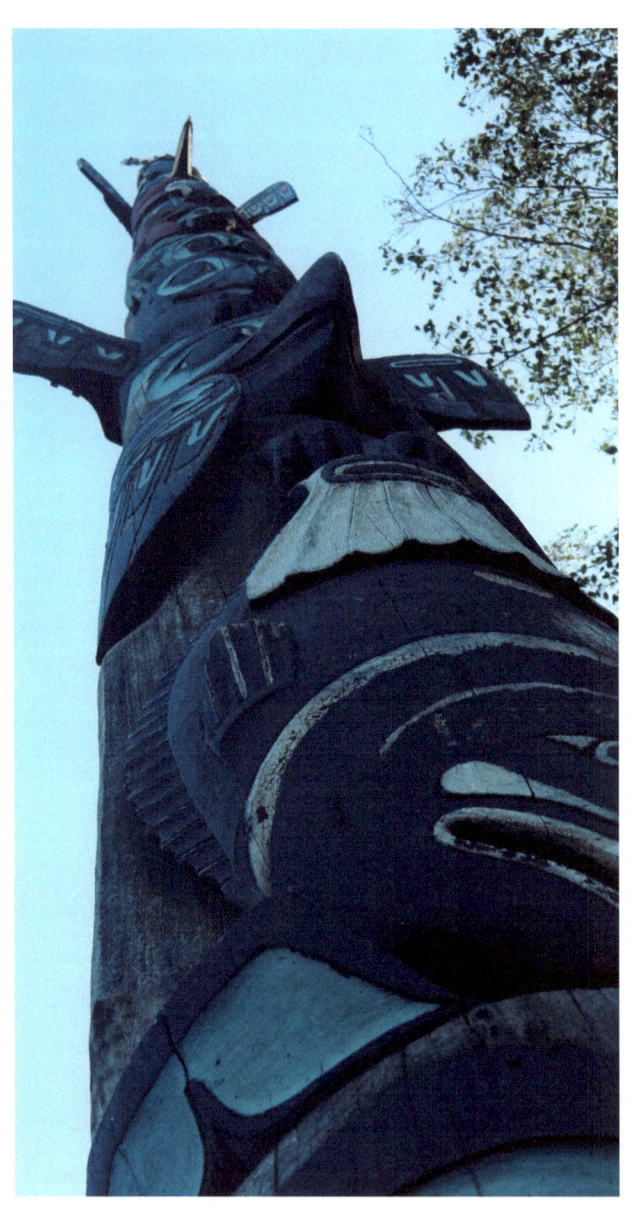

Pole on the Point

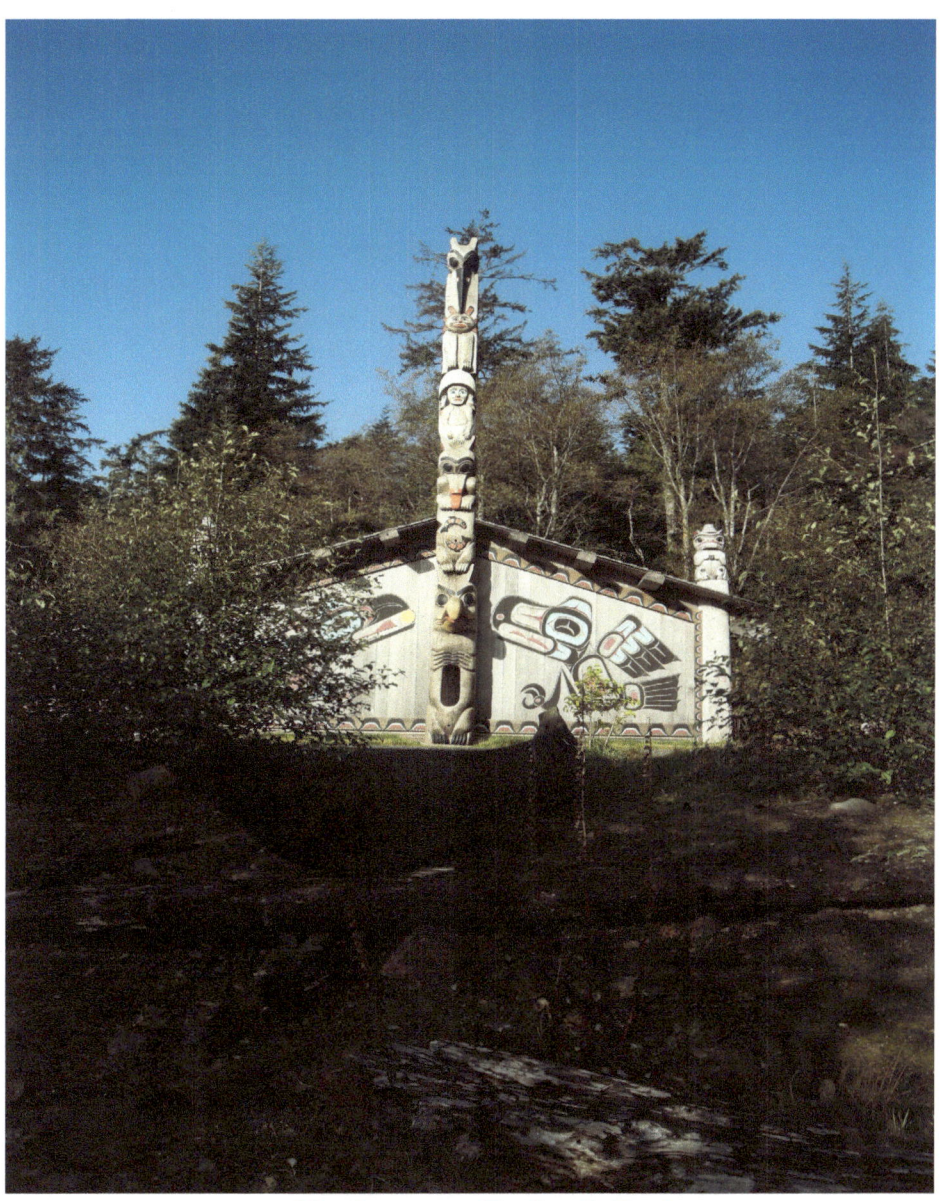

Clanhouse at Potlatch Park

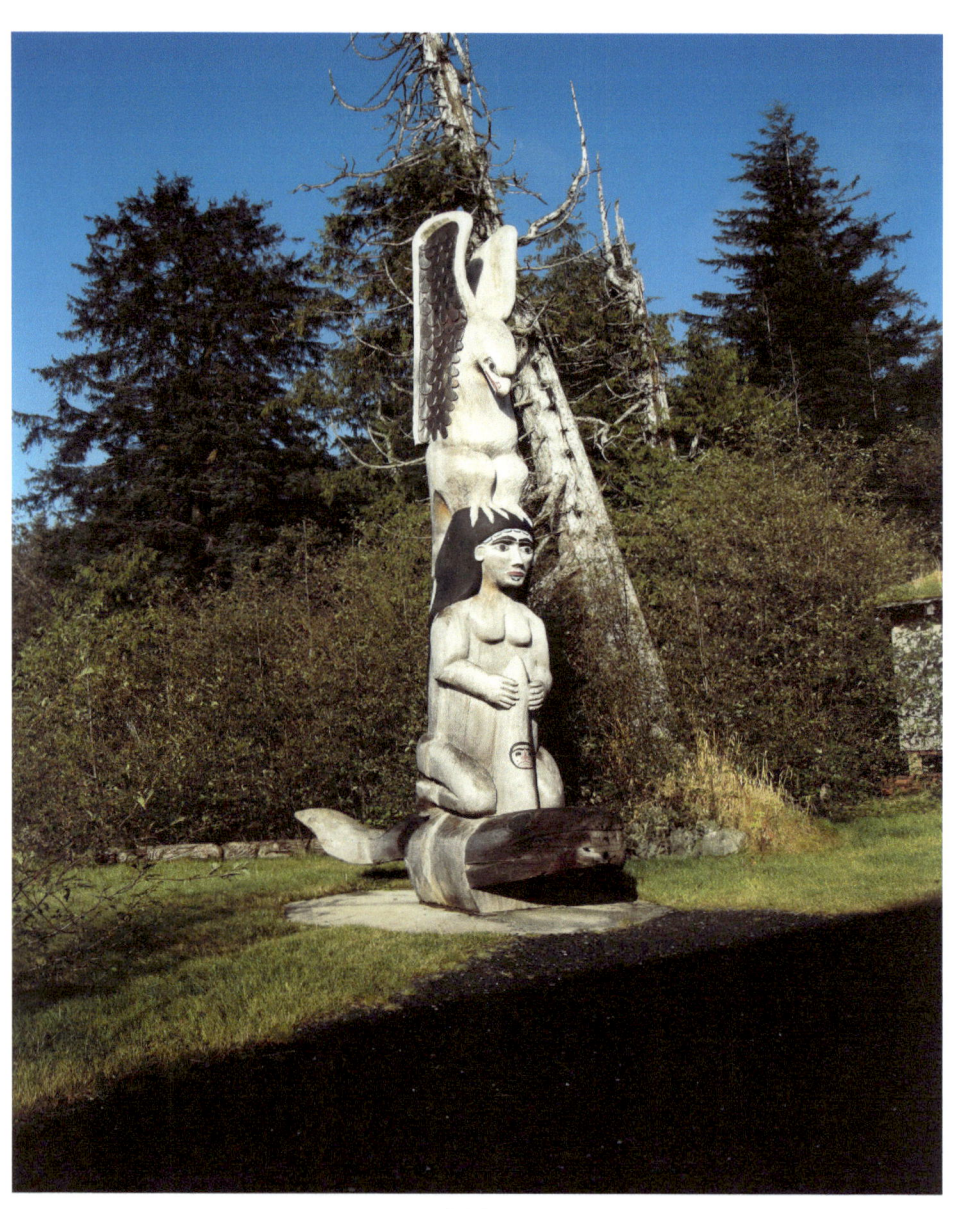

???

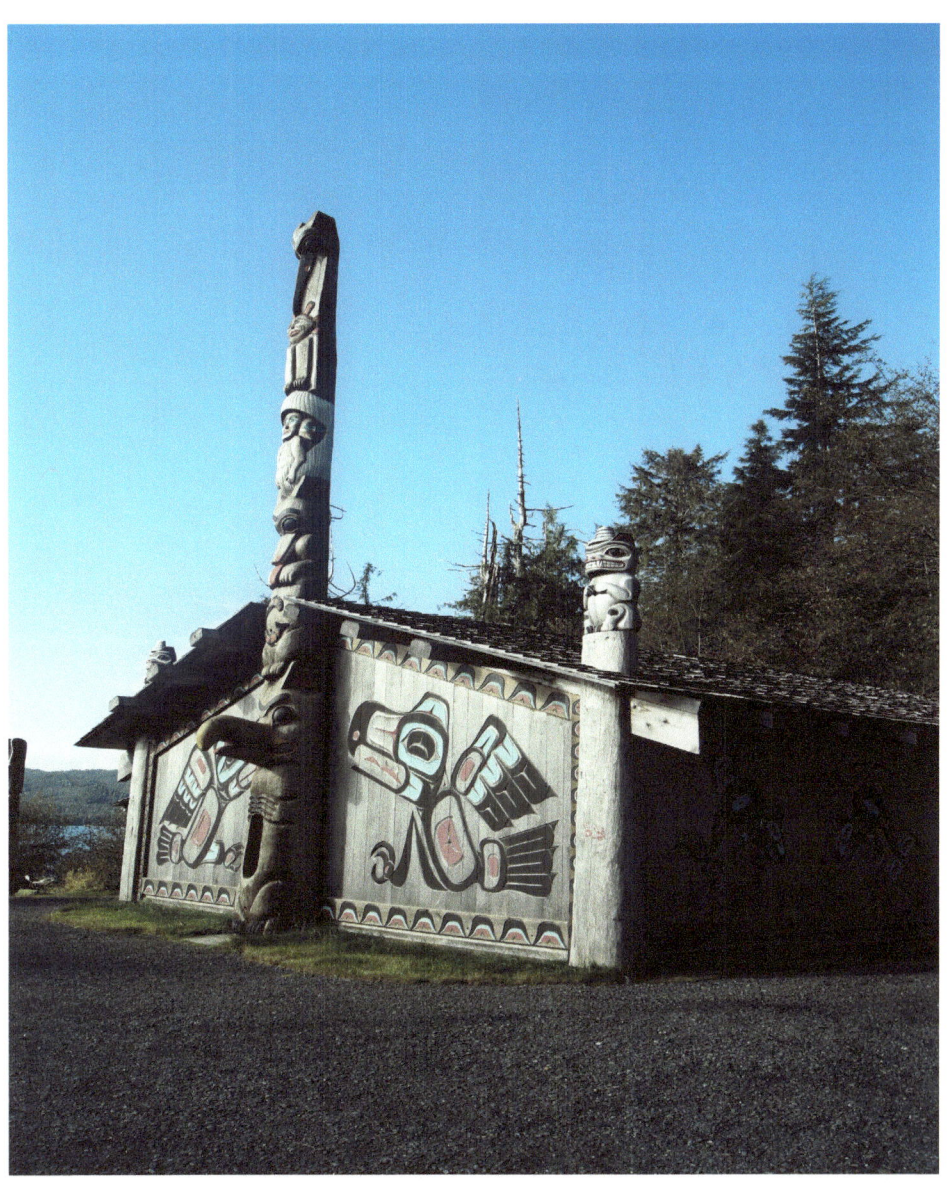

Clanhouse at Potlatch Park

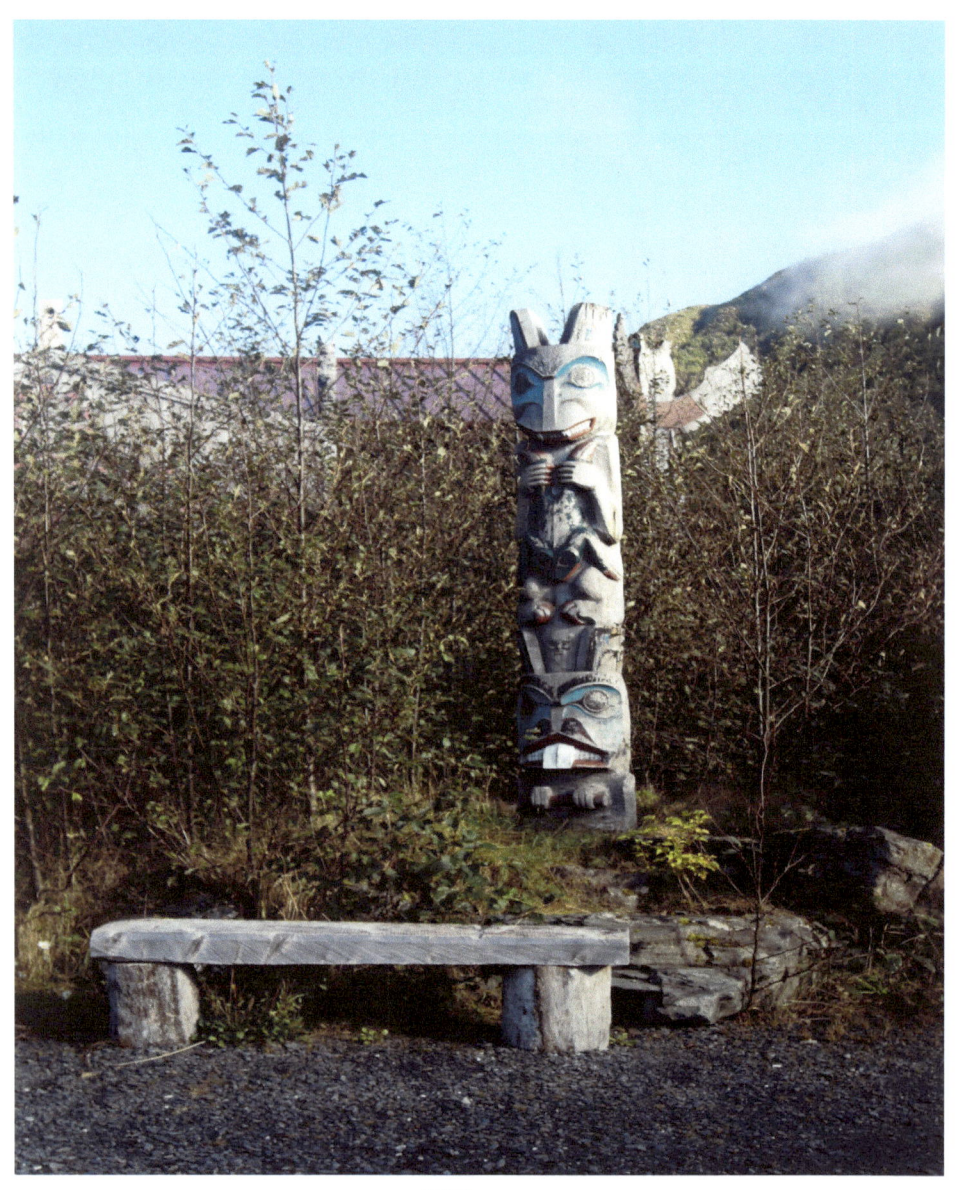

???

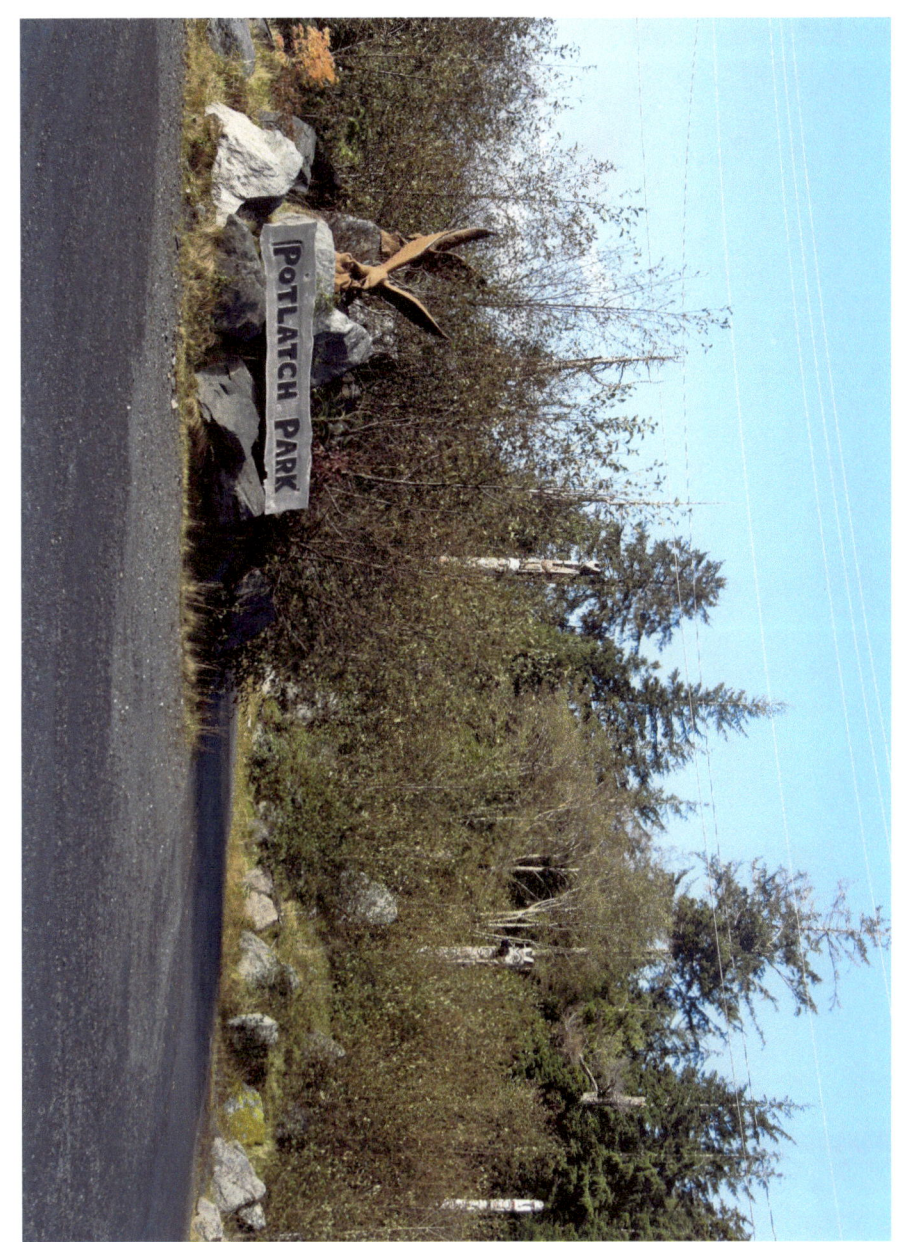

Totem Bight

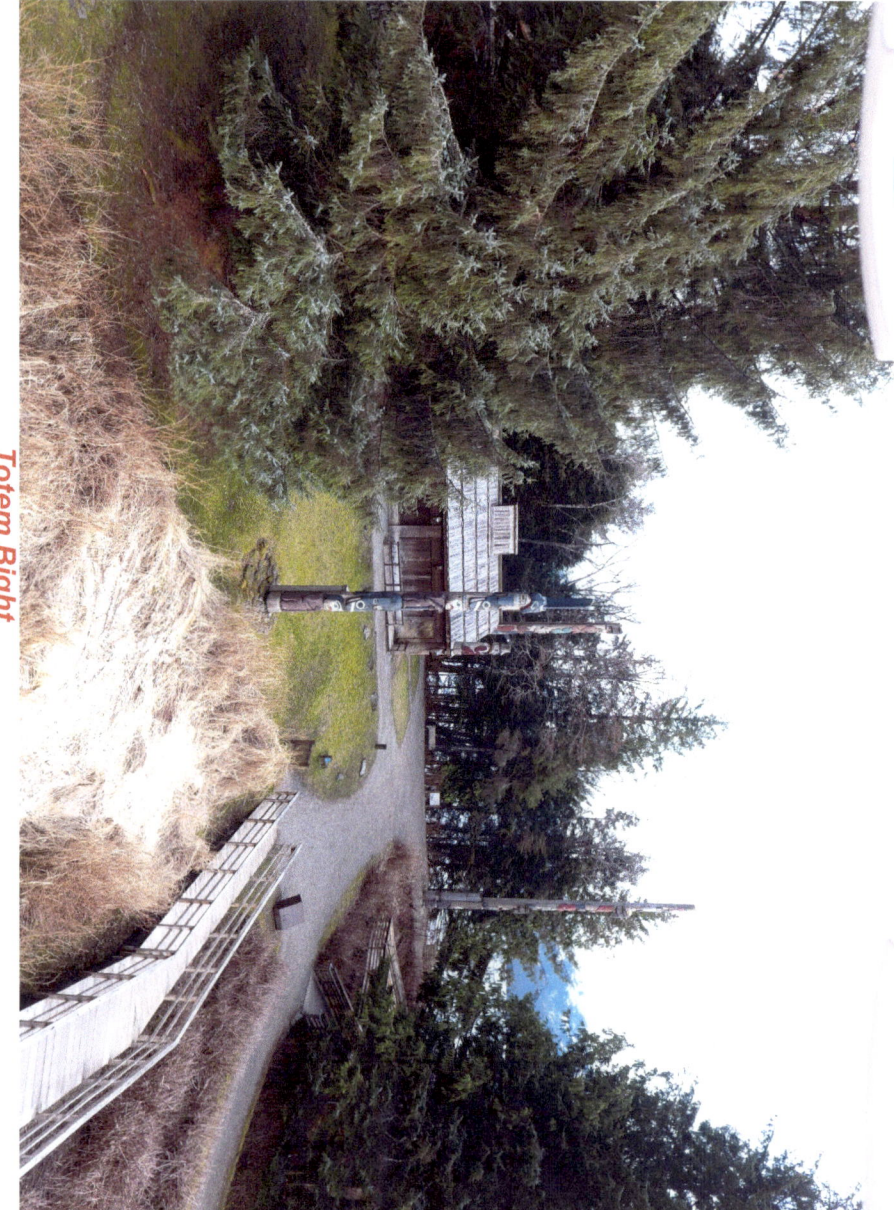

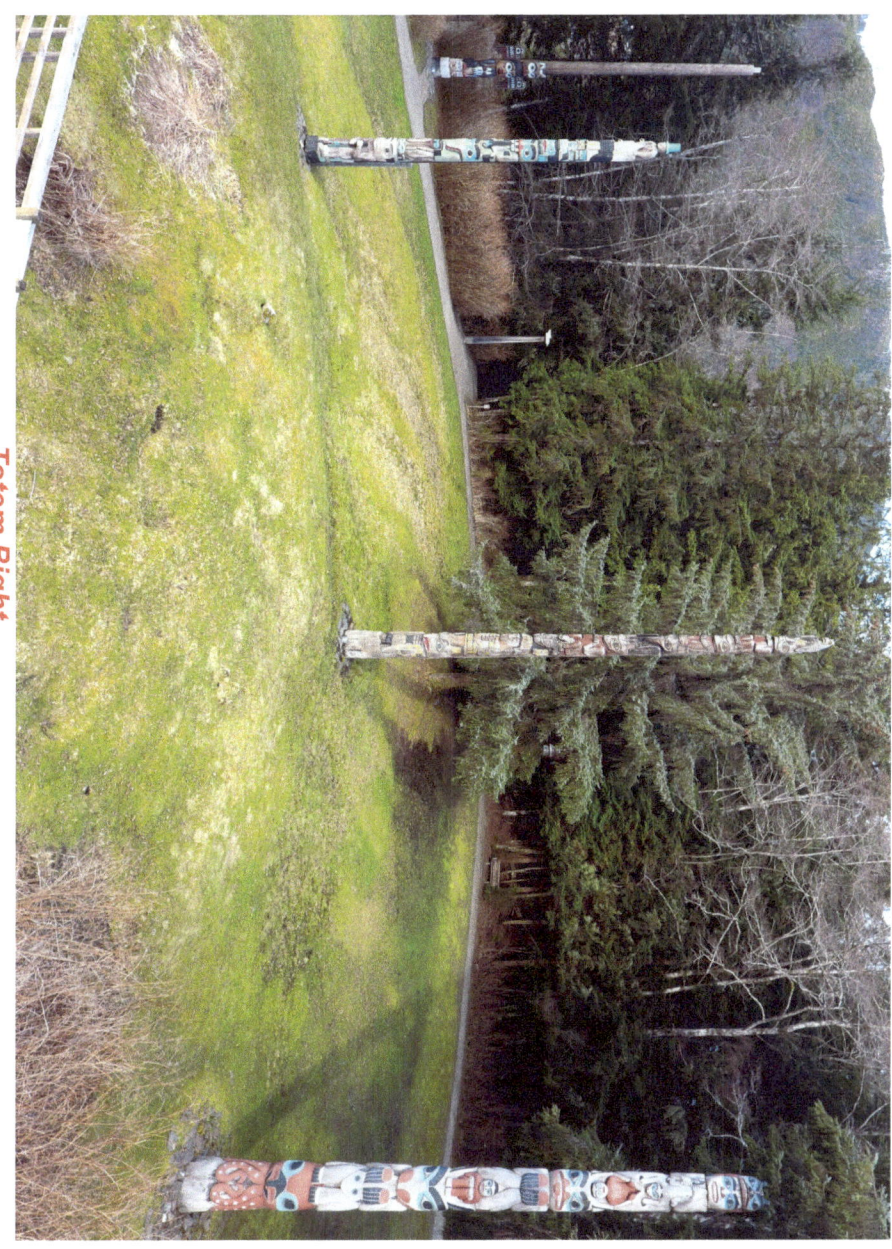

Totem Bight

Totem Bight Clan house

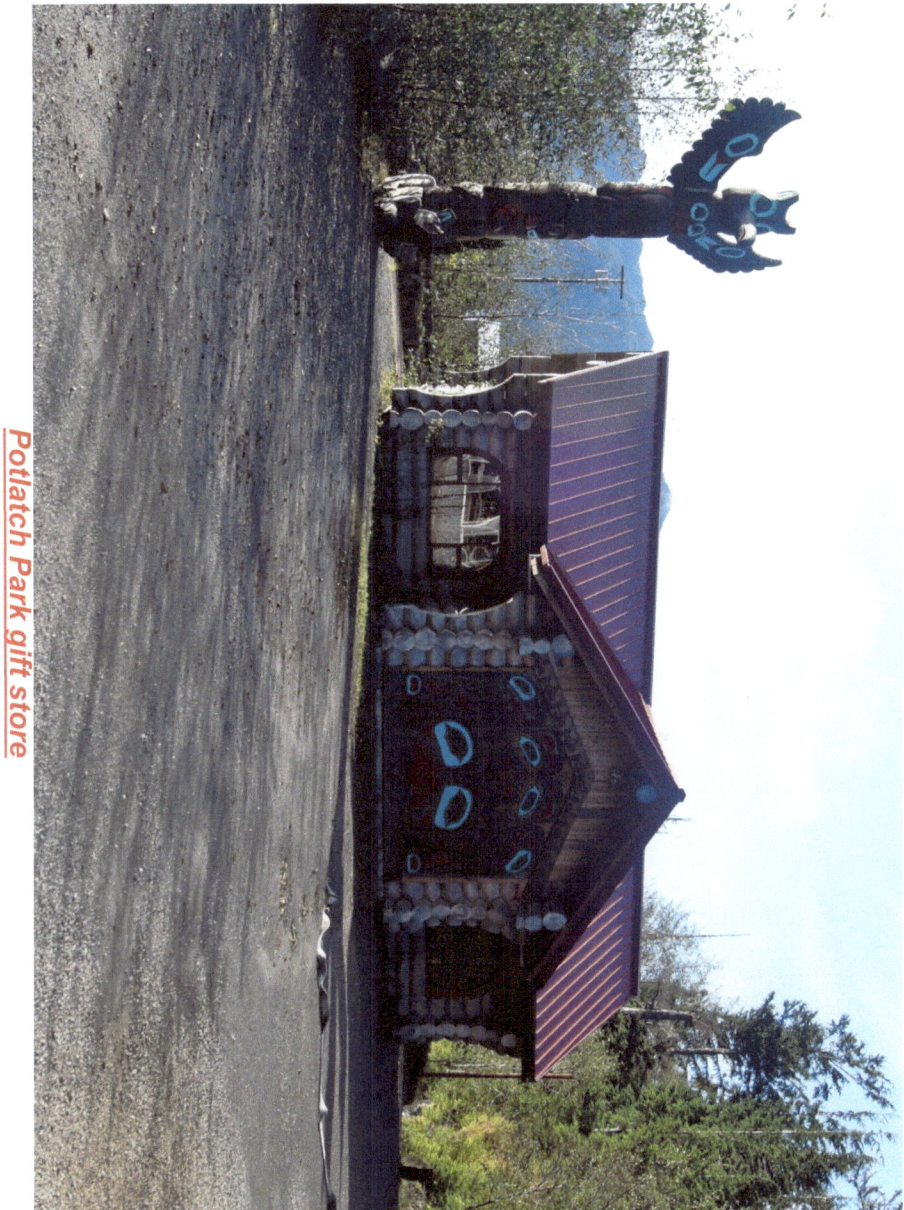

Potlatch Park gift store

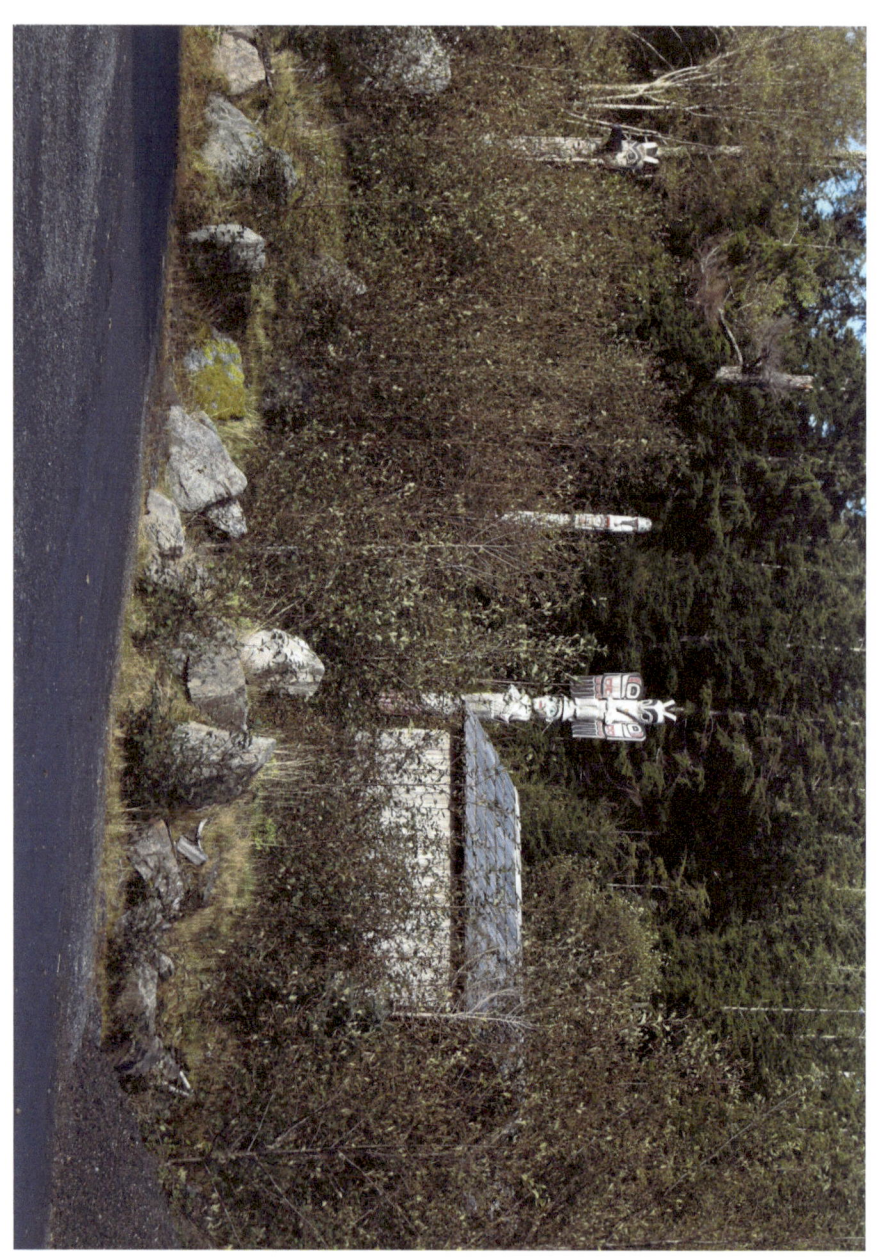

Potlatch park

Potlatch park

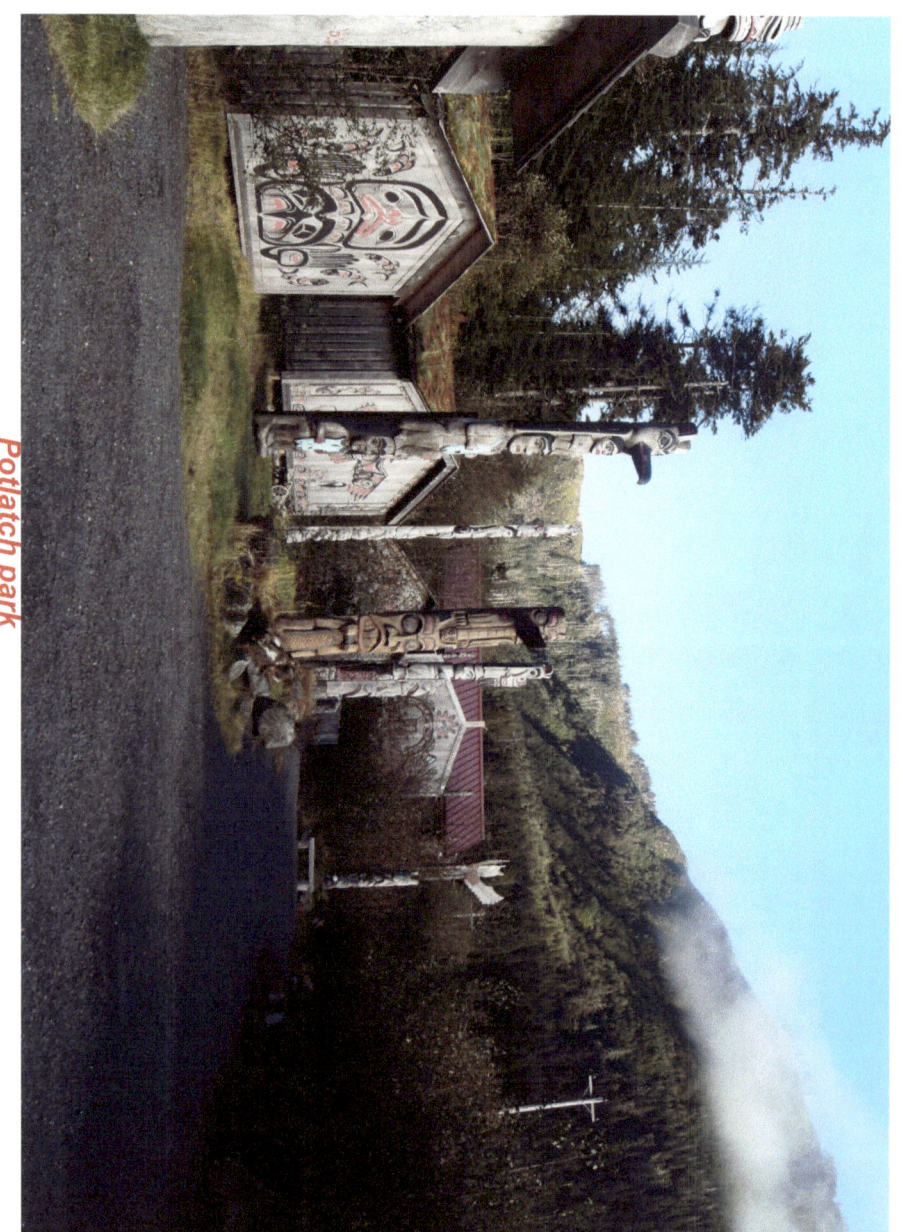

Potlatch park

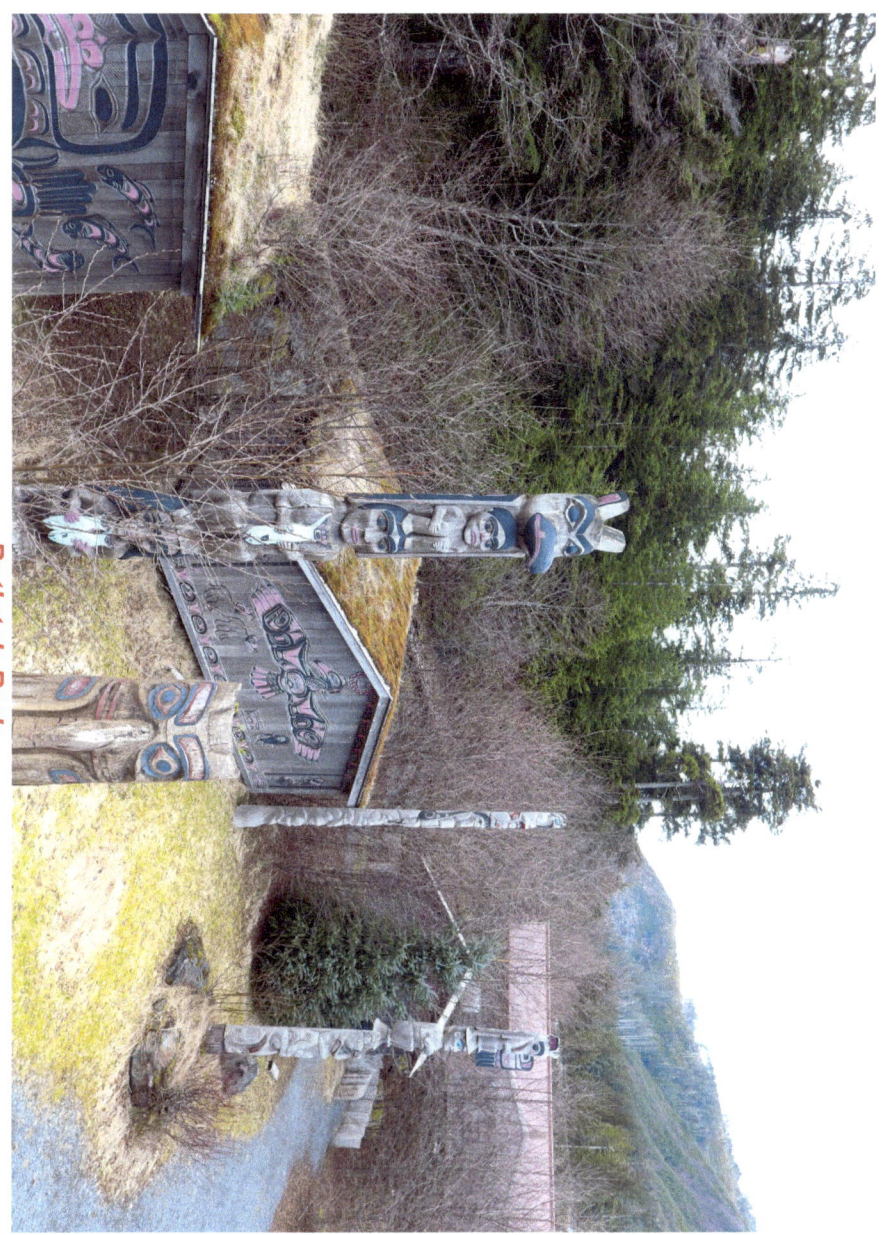

Potlatch Park

Totem Bight

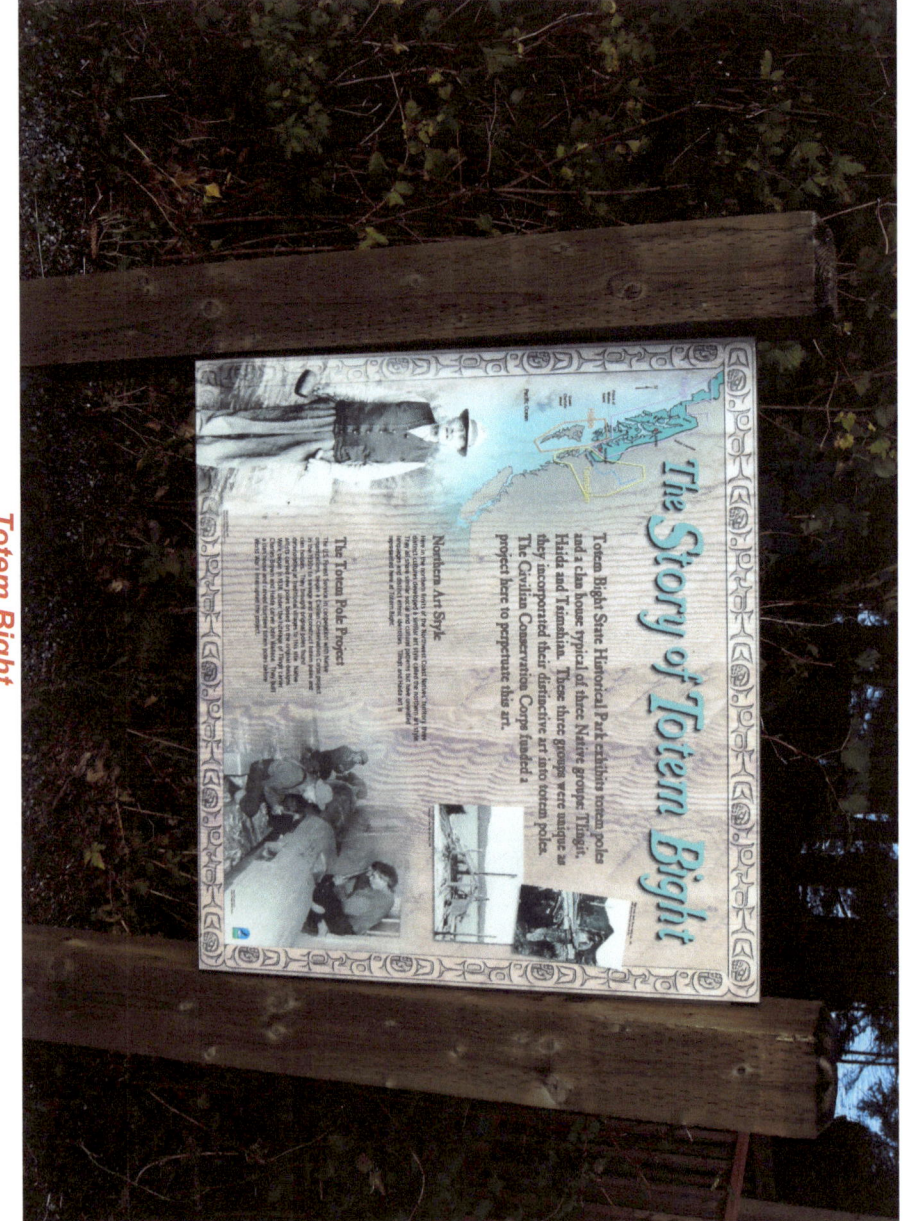

Totem Bight

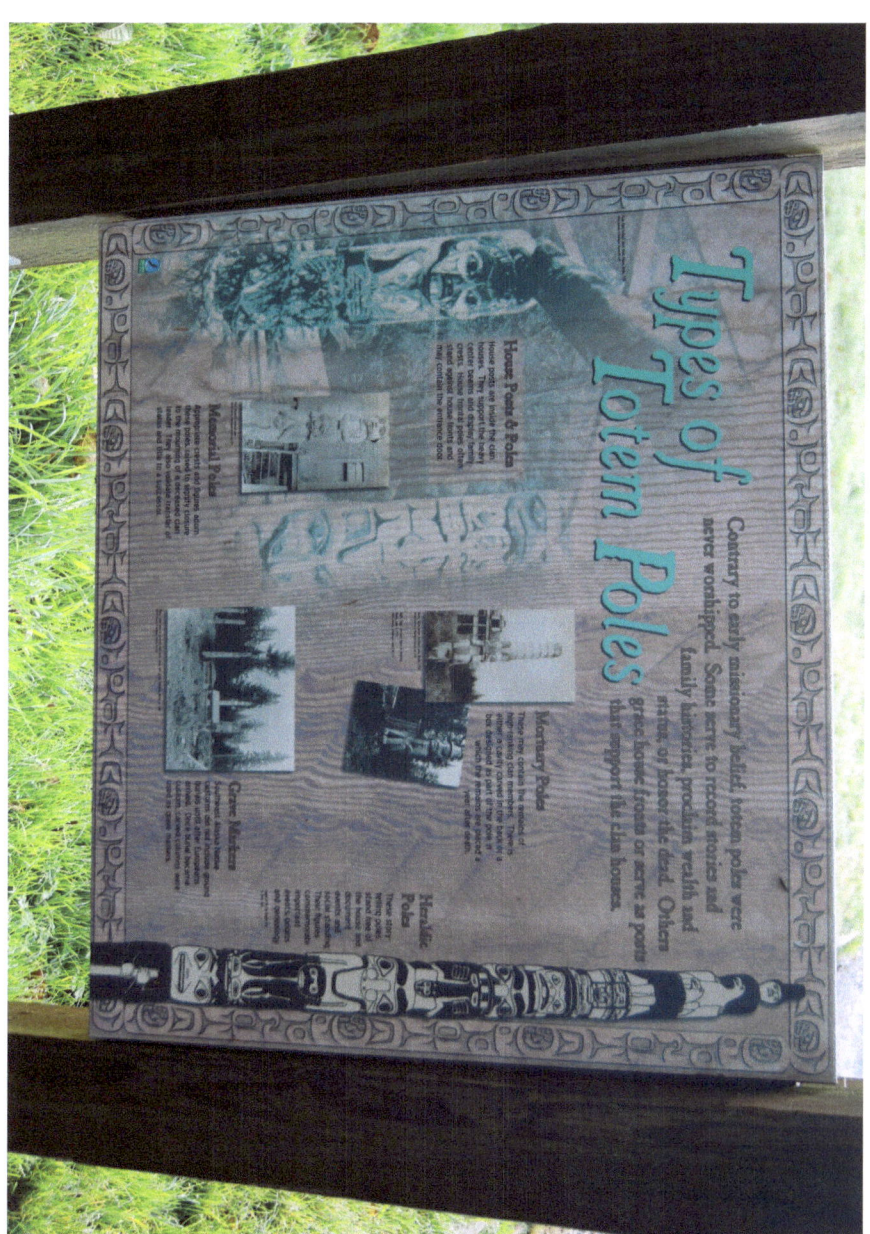

Totem Bight

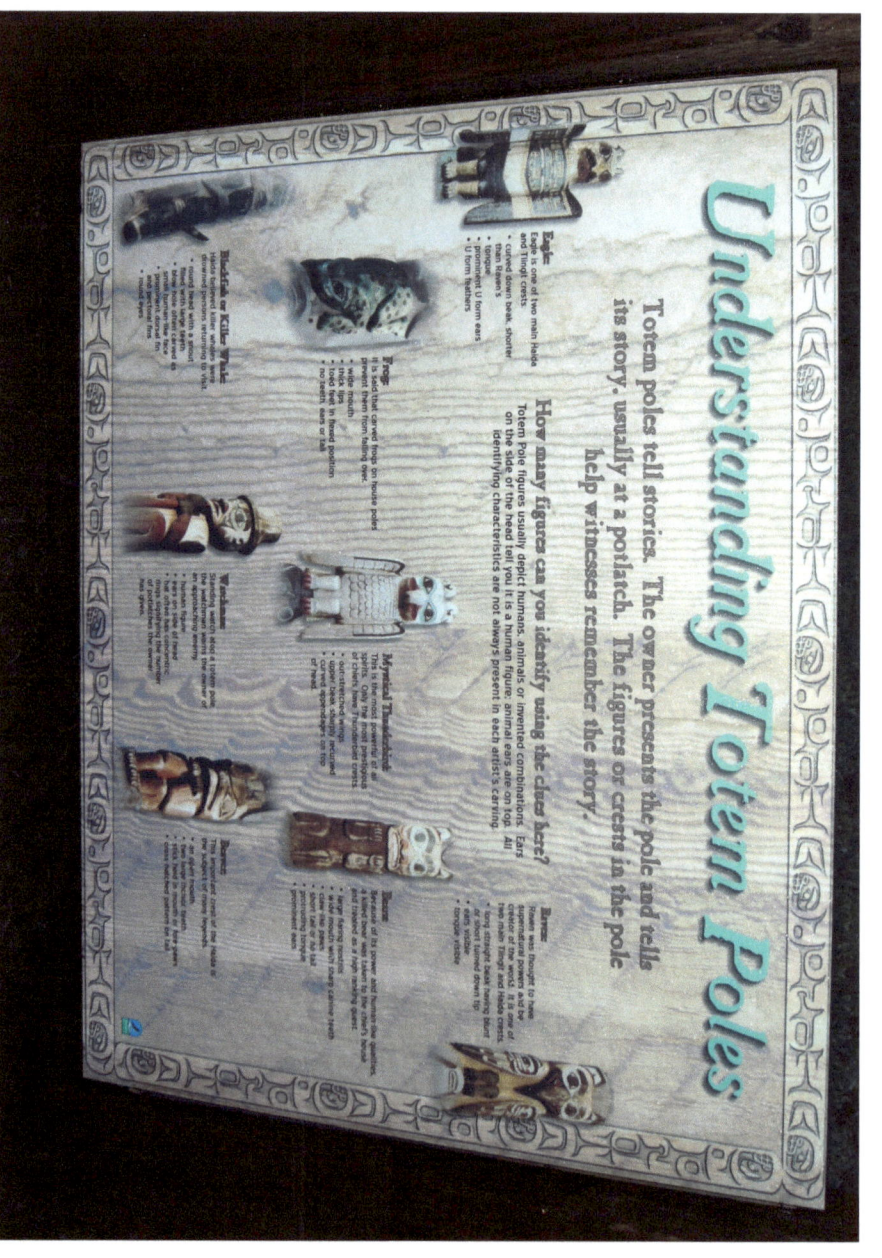

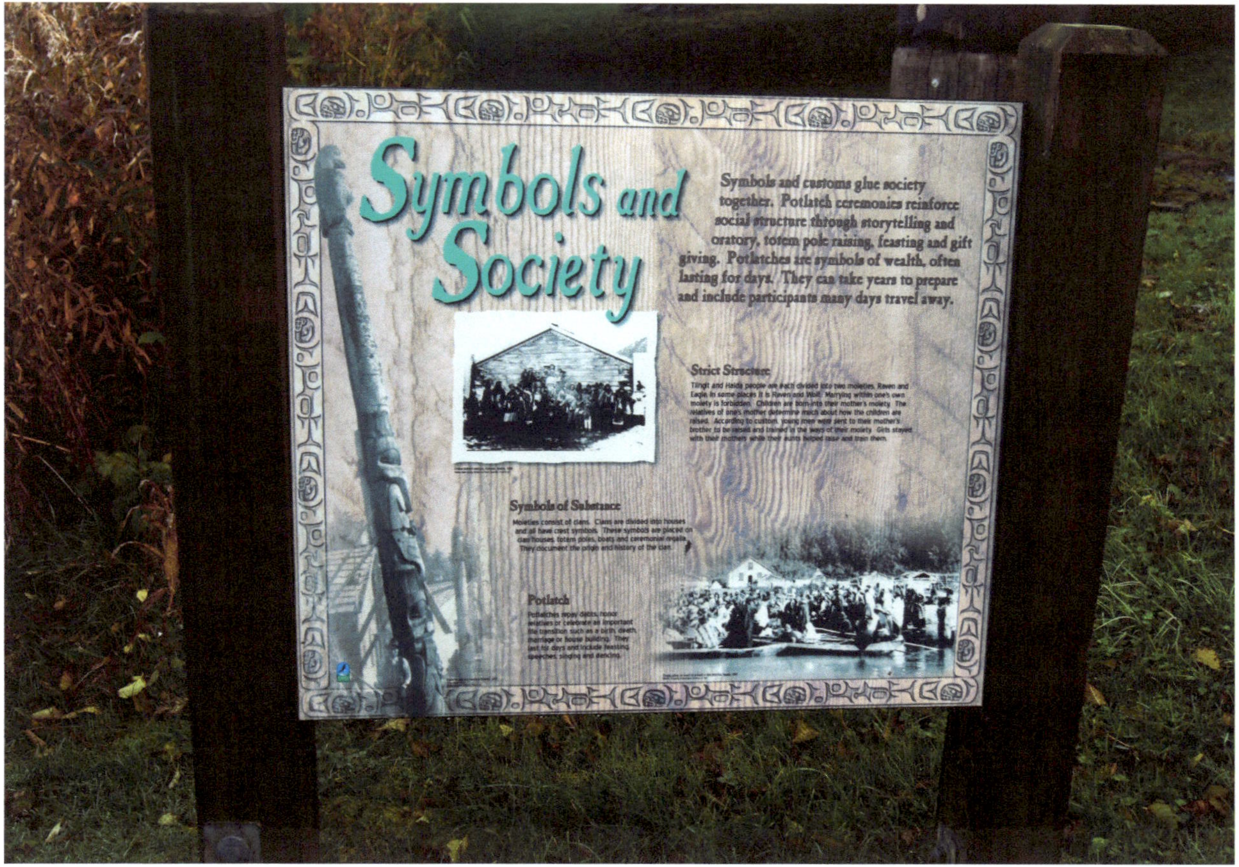
Symbols and Society
Symbols and customs glue society together. Potlatch ceremonies reinforce social structure through storytelling and oratory, totem pole raising, feasting and gift giving. Potlatches are symbols of wealth, often lasting for days. They can take years to prepare and include participants many days travel away.
Strict Structure
Tlingit and Haida people are each divided into two moieties, Raven and Eagle. In some places it is Raven and Wolf. Marrying within one's own moiety is forbidden. Children are born into their mother's moiety. The relatives of one's mother determine much about how the children are raised. According to custom, young men were sent to their mother's brother to be raised and trained in the ways of their moiety. Girls stayed with their mothers while their aunts helped raise and train them.
Symbols of Substance
Moieties consist of clans. Clans are divided into houses and all have crest symbols. These symbols are placed on clan houses, totem poles, boats and ceremonial regalia. They document the origin and history of the clan.
Potlatch
Potlatches repay debts, honor relatives or celebrate an important life transition such as a birth, death, marriage or house building. They last for days and include feasting, speeches, singing and dancing.

Totem Bight

Totem Bight

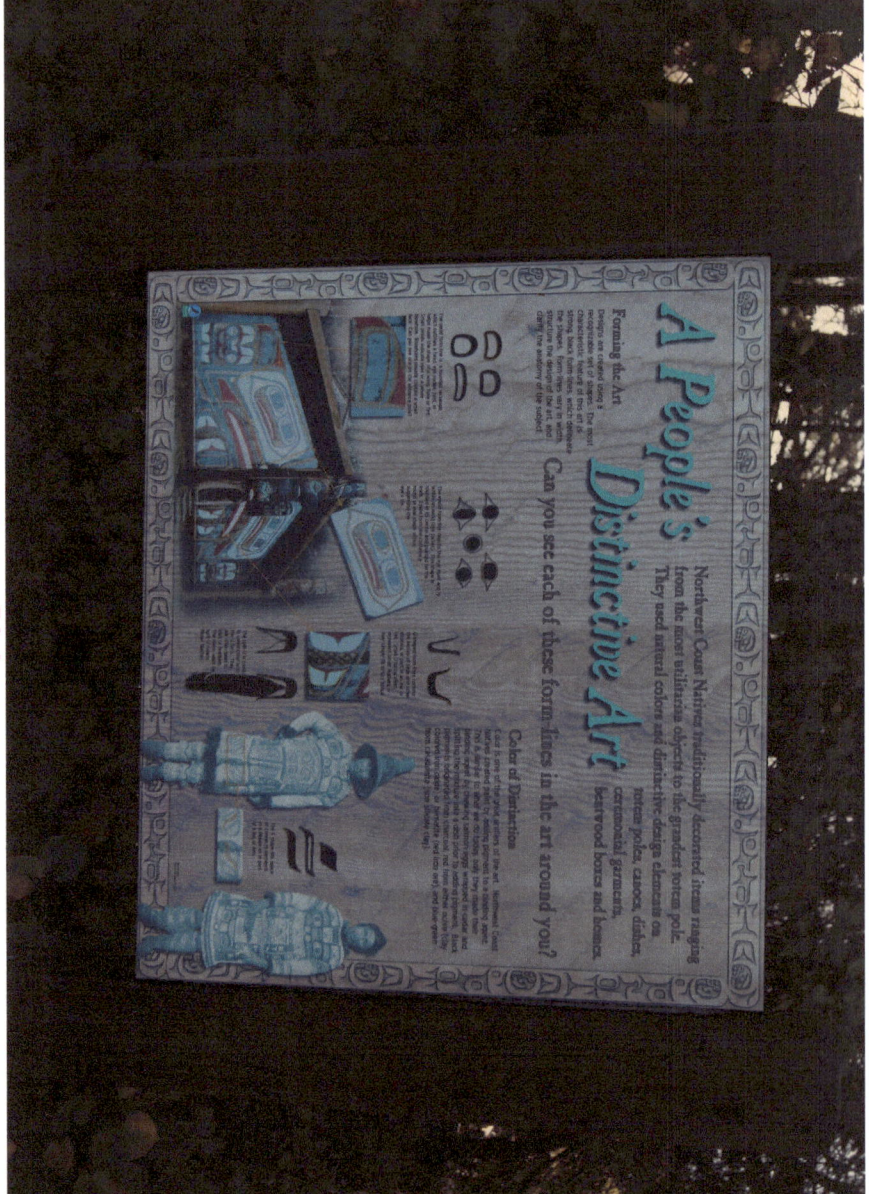

Totem Bight

A Look Into the Clan House

Twenty to fifty closely related clan members lived together working, eating and sleeping under one roof. Let's look back a couple hundred years and see what life was like inside a clan house.

A Warrior's Home

Look Around

Watch Your Head

Totem Bight

Transforming Trees

Native carvers took large western red cedar and transformed them into magnificent totem poles.

Traditional Tools

Raising a Monument

Respect for the Totem Trees

Saxman

**2706 S Tongass
5 acres
Admission $5 a person
Last count 29 poles**

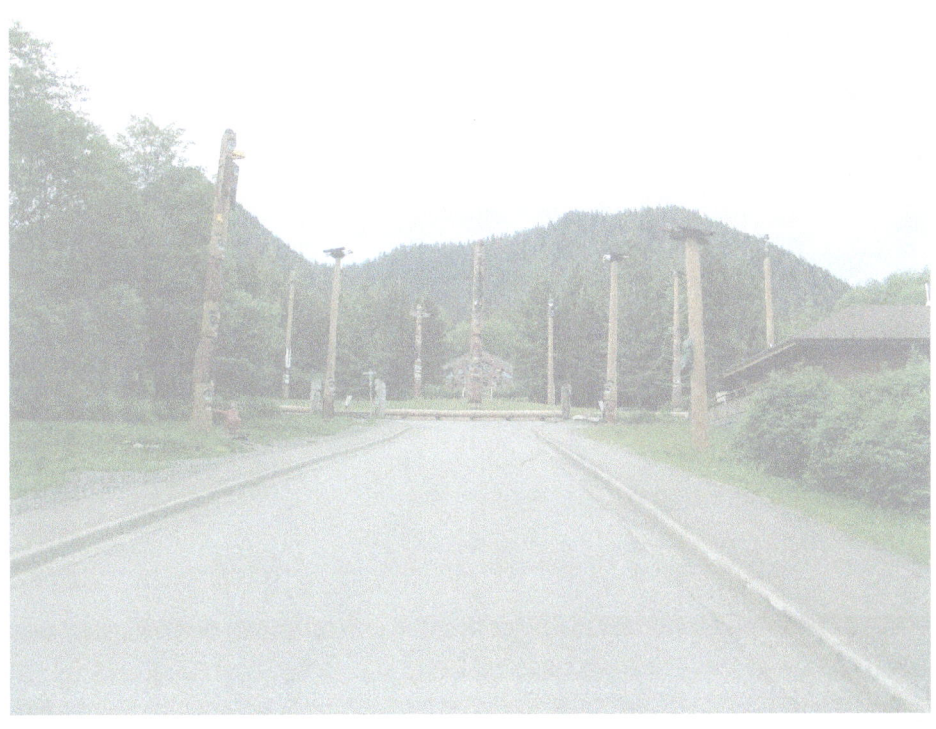

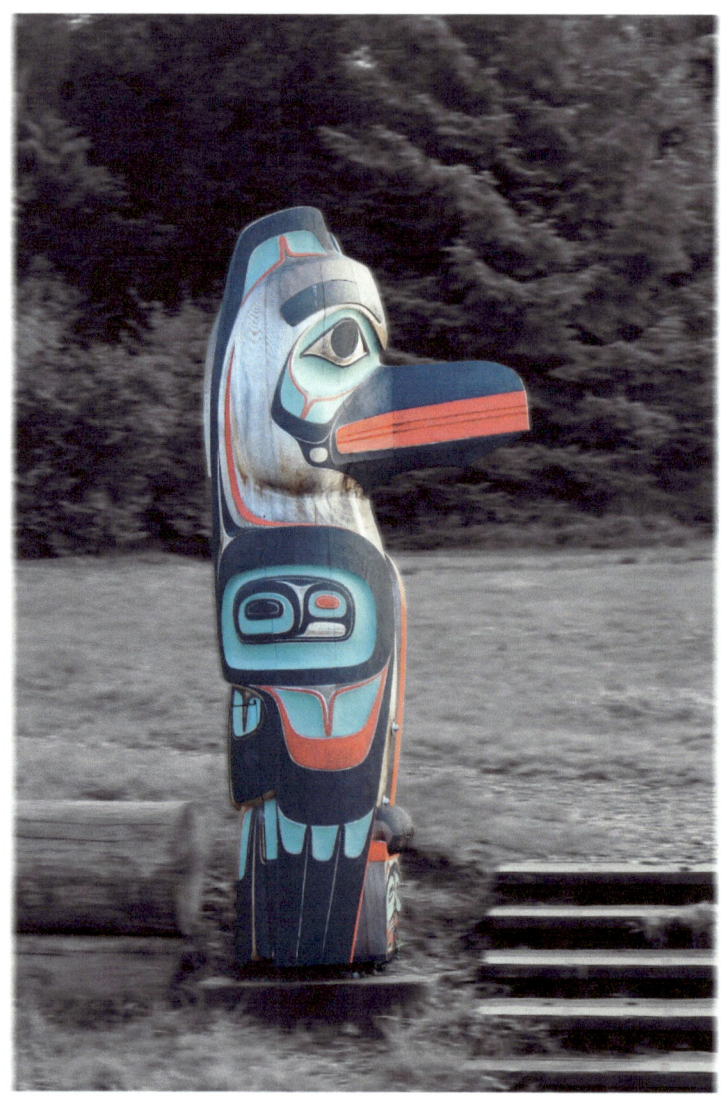

Totem Guard

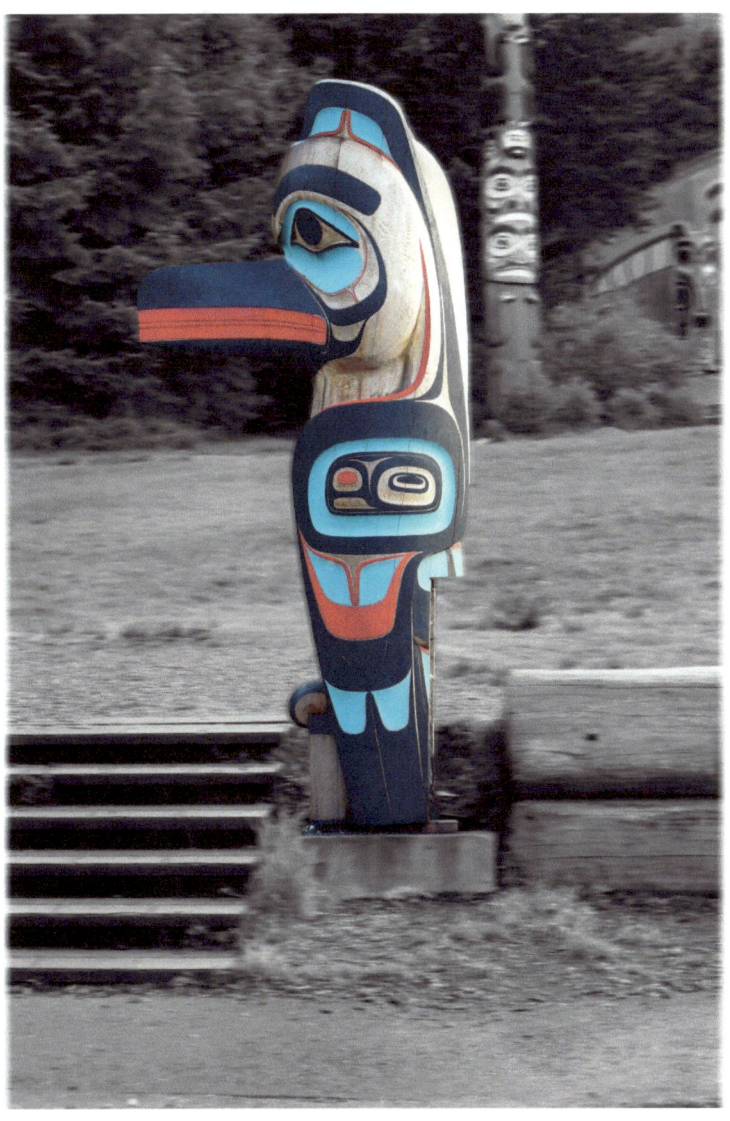

Totem Guard

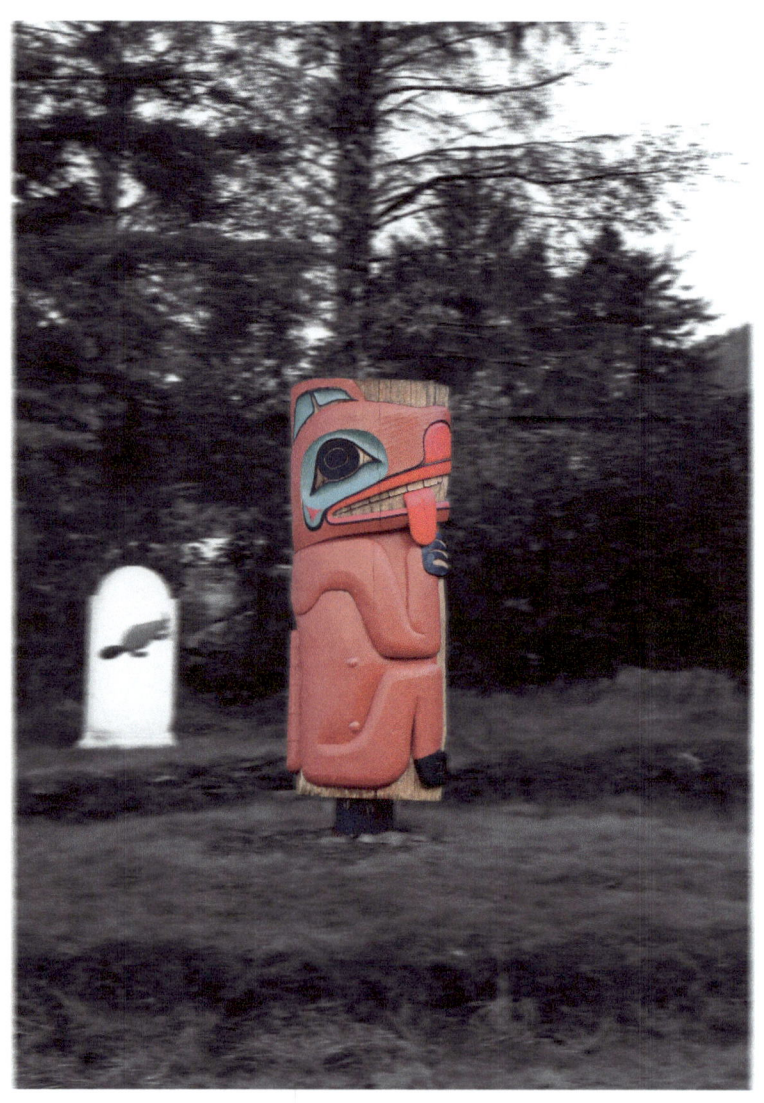

Tired Wolf House Post

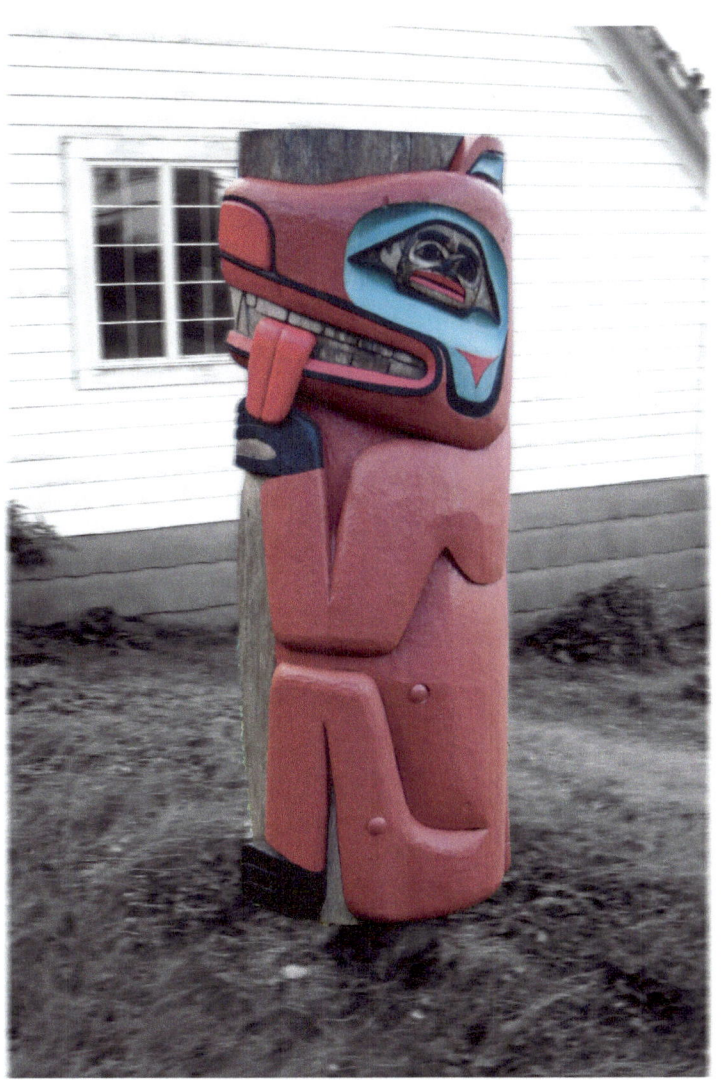

Tired Wolf House Post

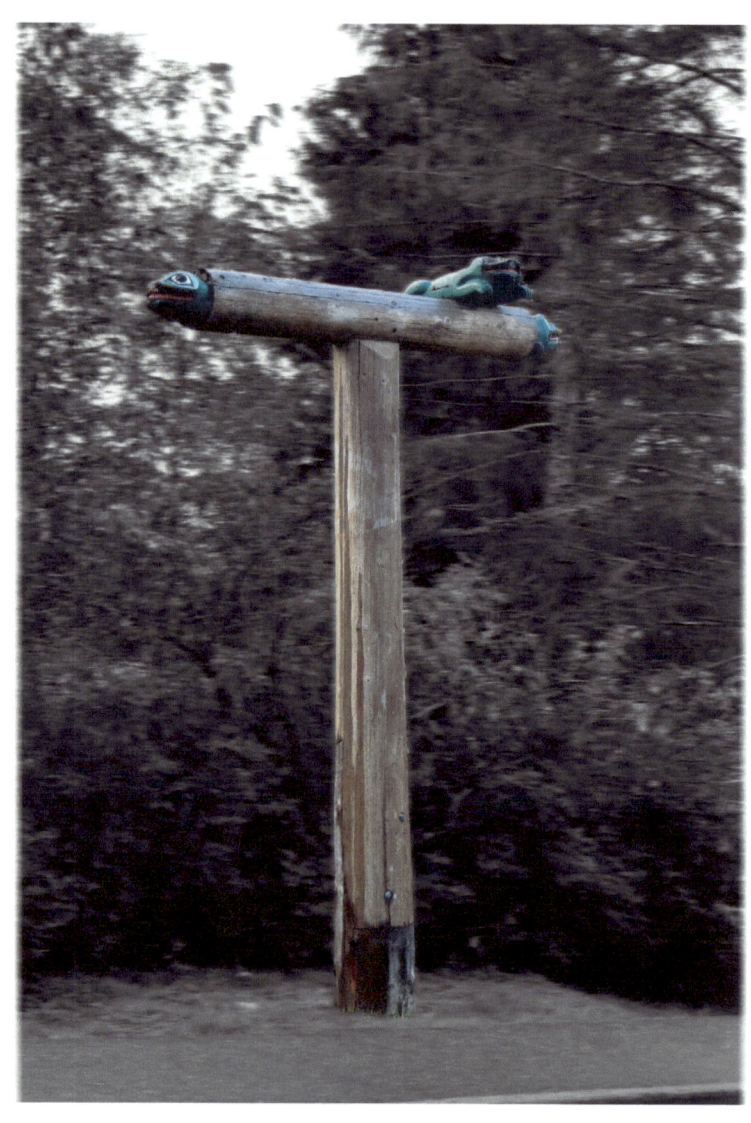

Two Frogs Pole

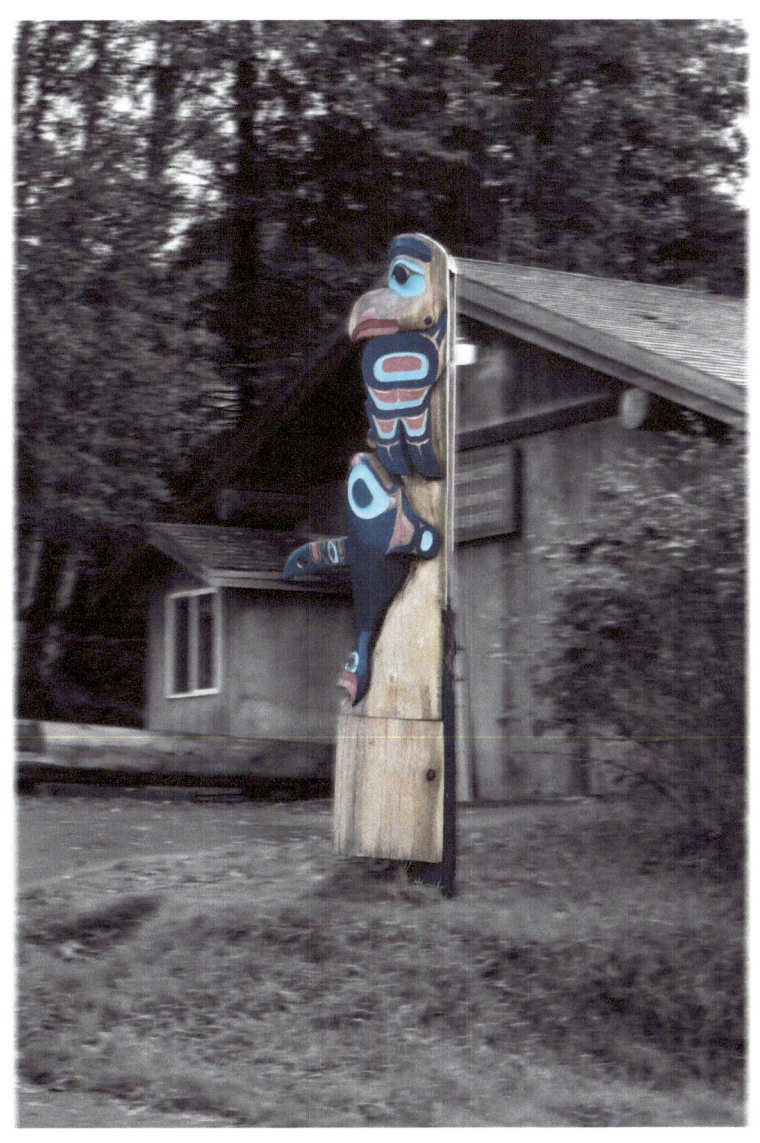
Whale Thunderbird Pole

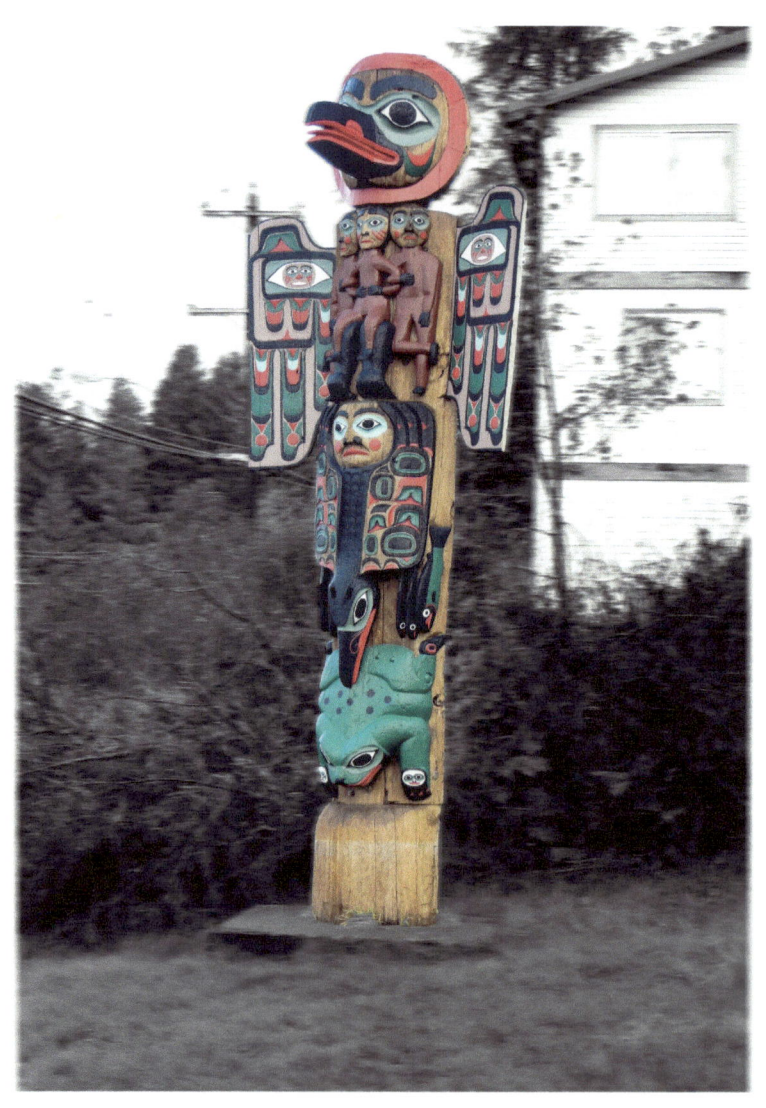

Sun Raven Pole

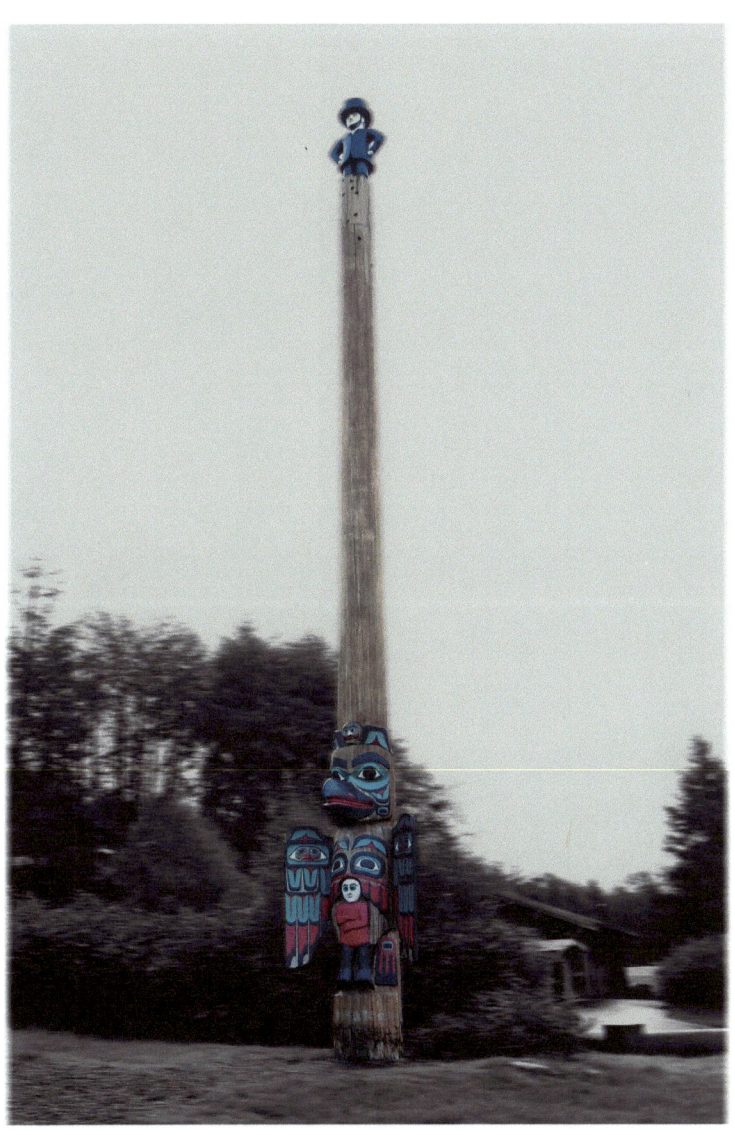

Lincoln Pole

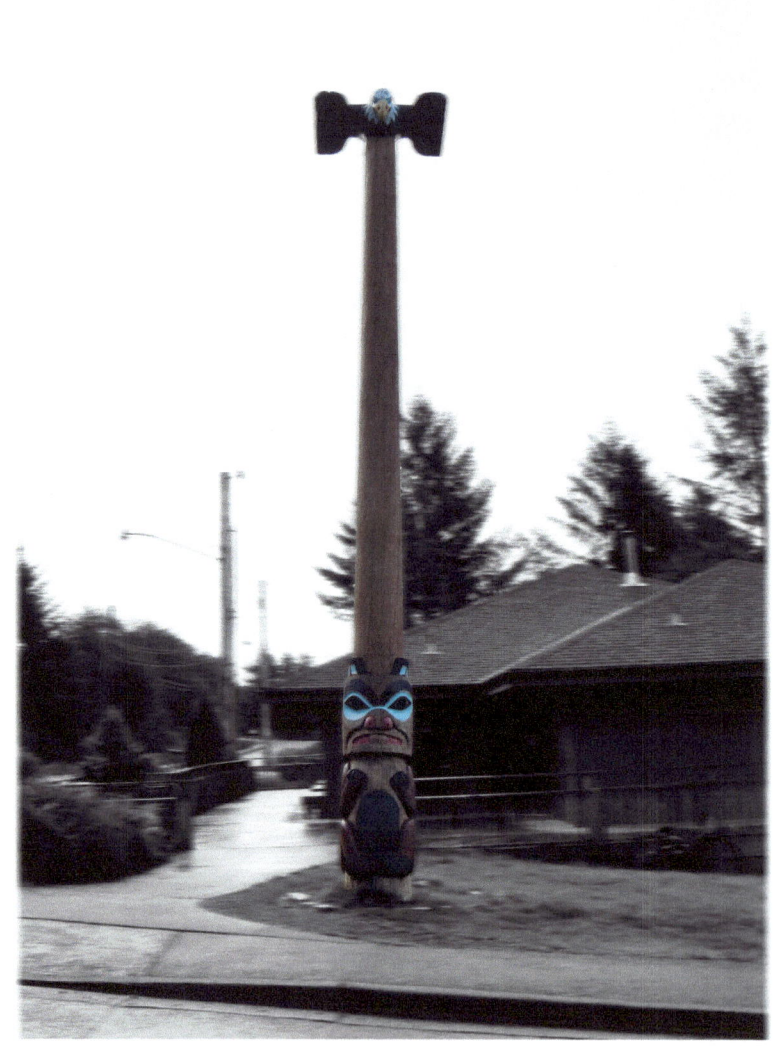

Eagle Beaver Pole

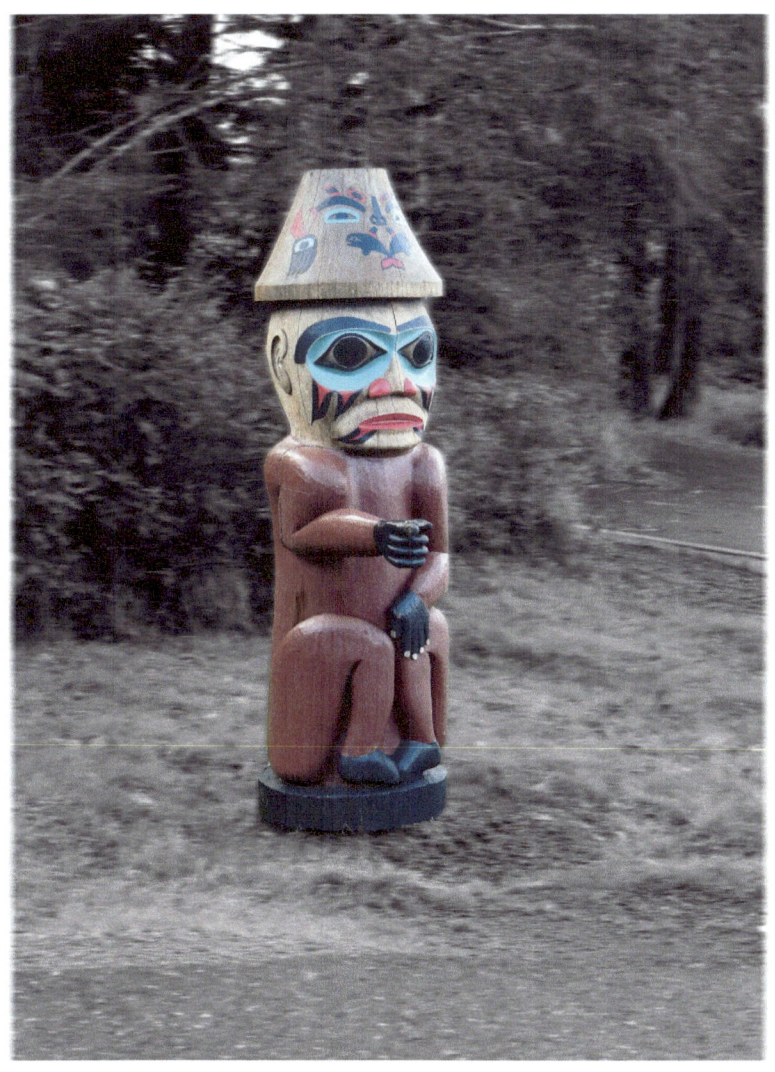

The Pointing Figure

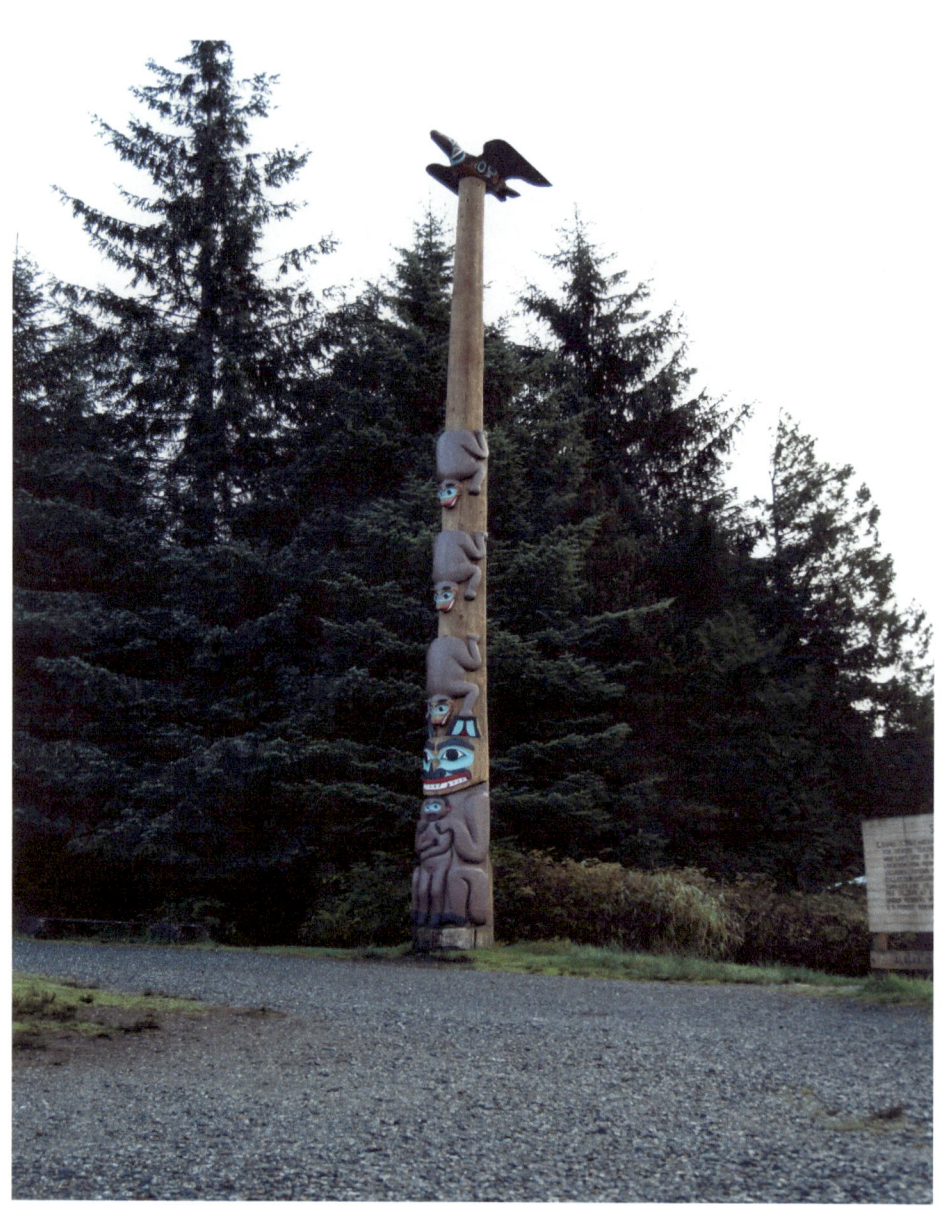

Kats/Loon Pole

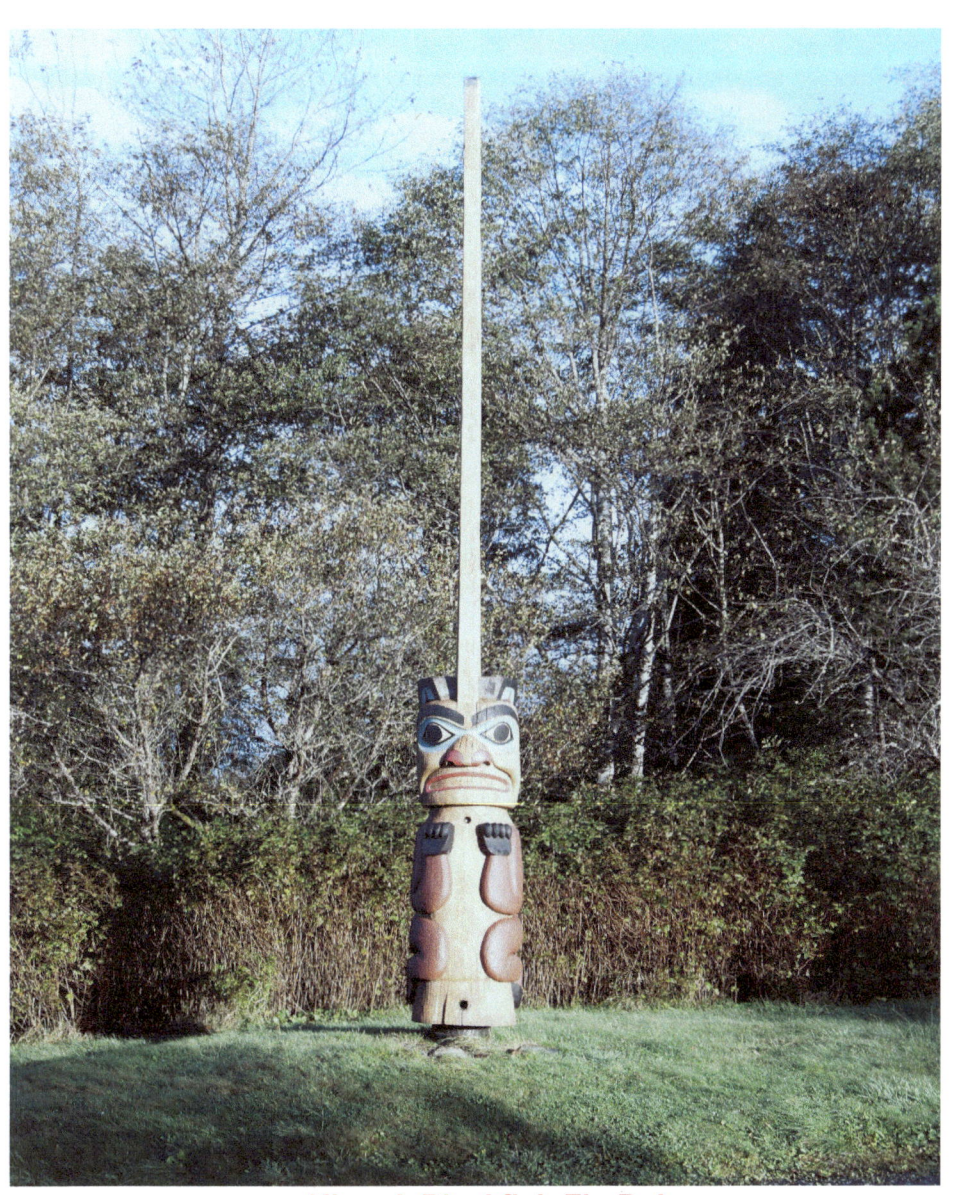

Klawak Blackfish Fin Pole

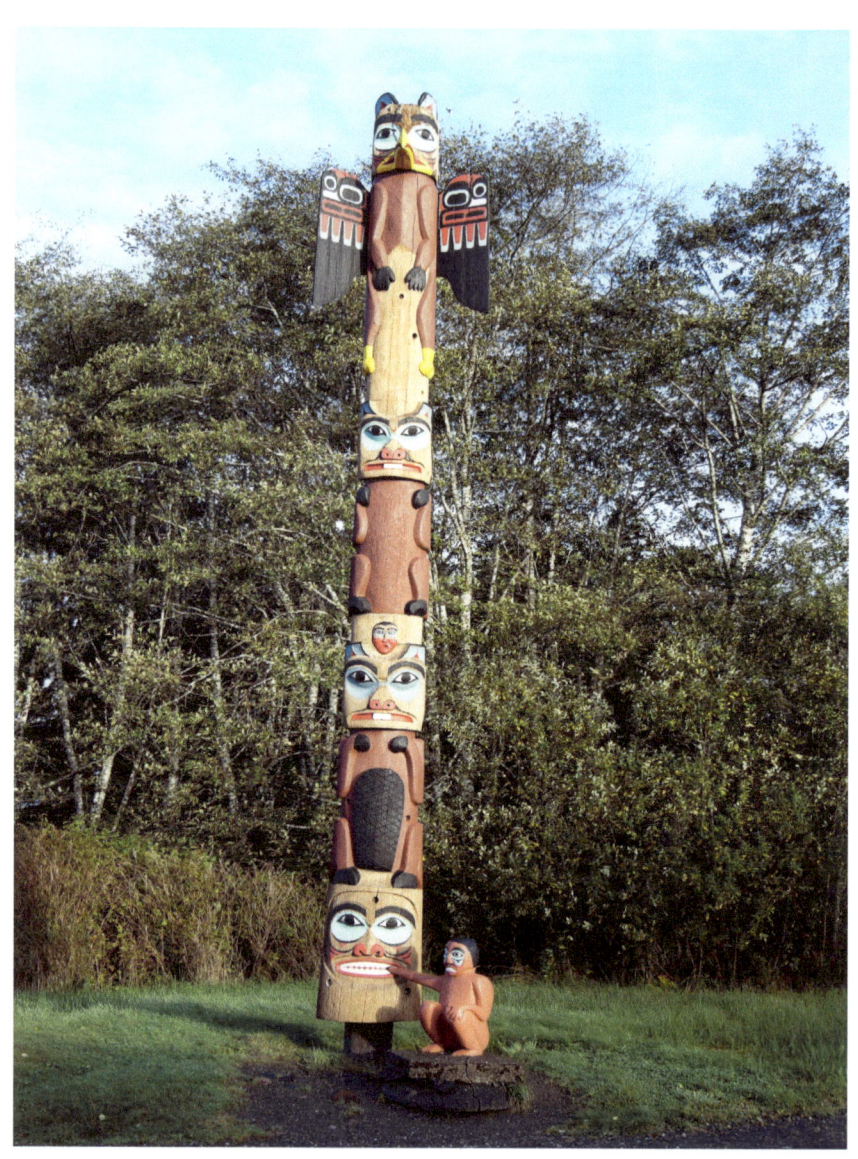

Rock Oysterman Pole

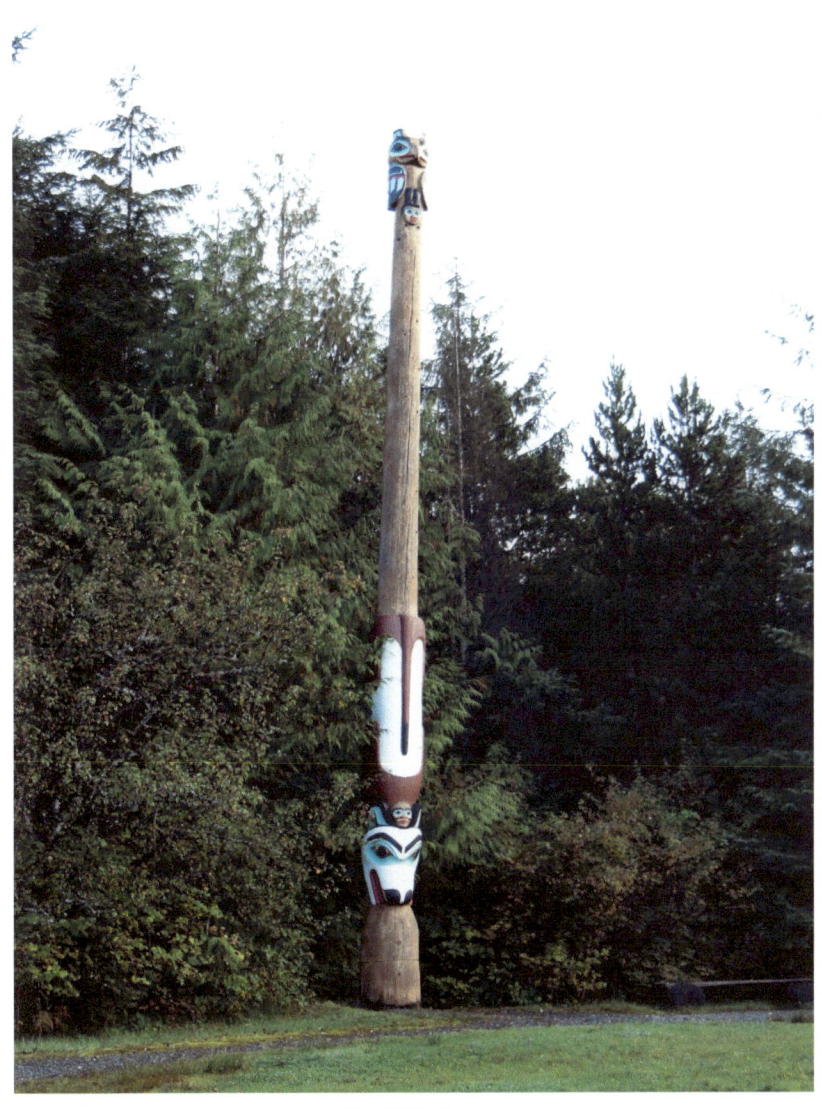

Owl Pole

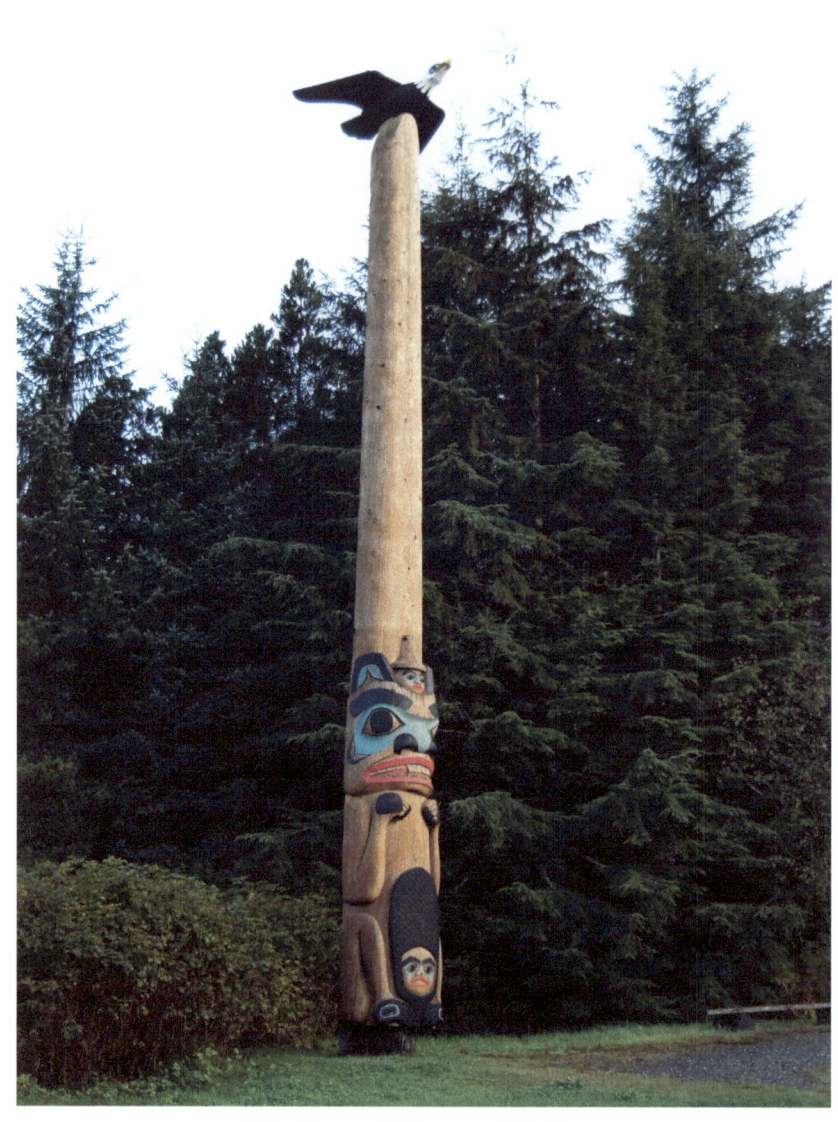

Eagle and Beaver Pole

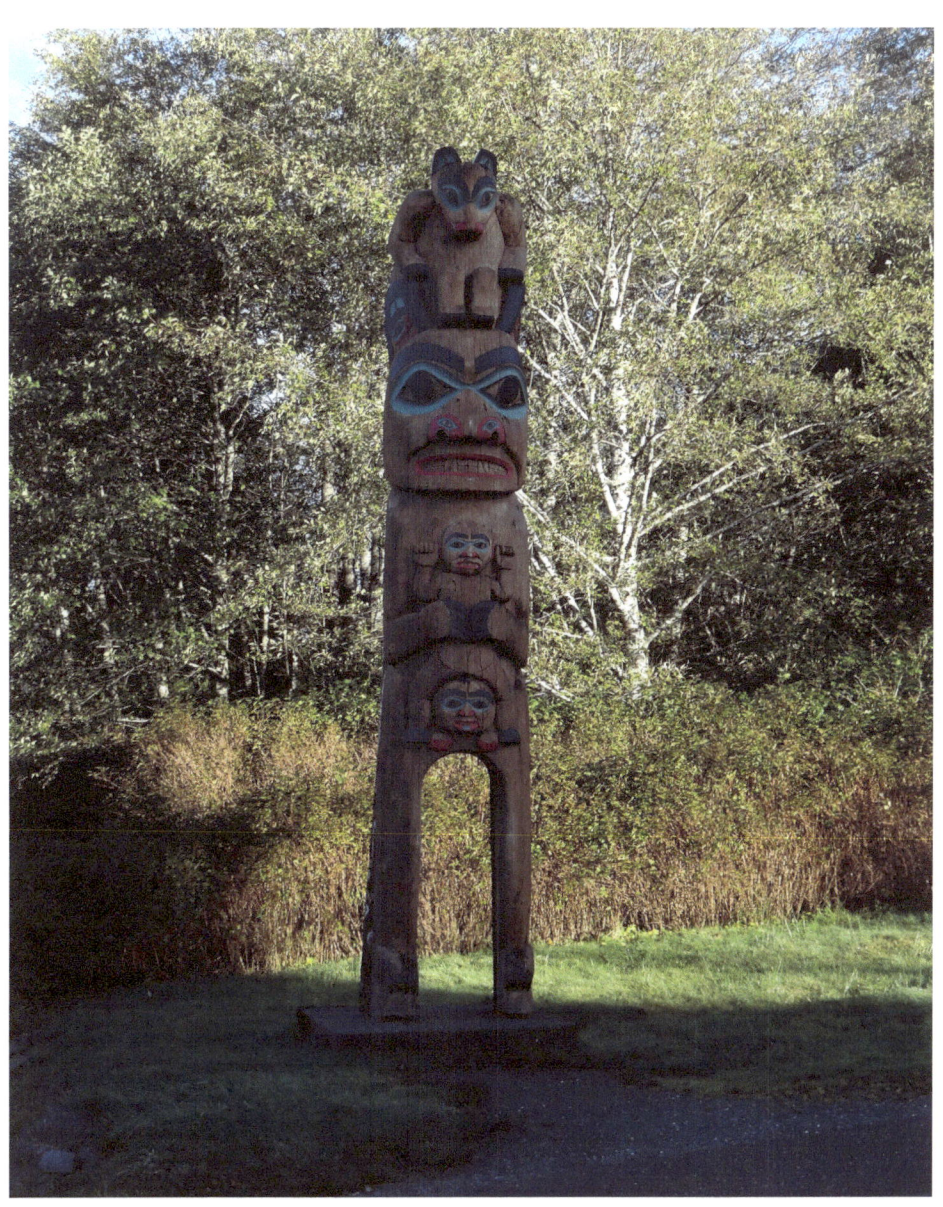

Kats and Bear Wife Pole

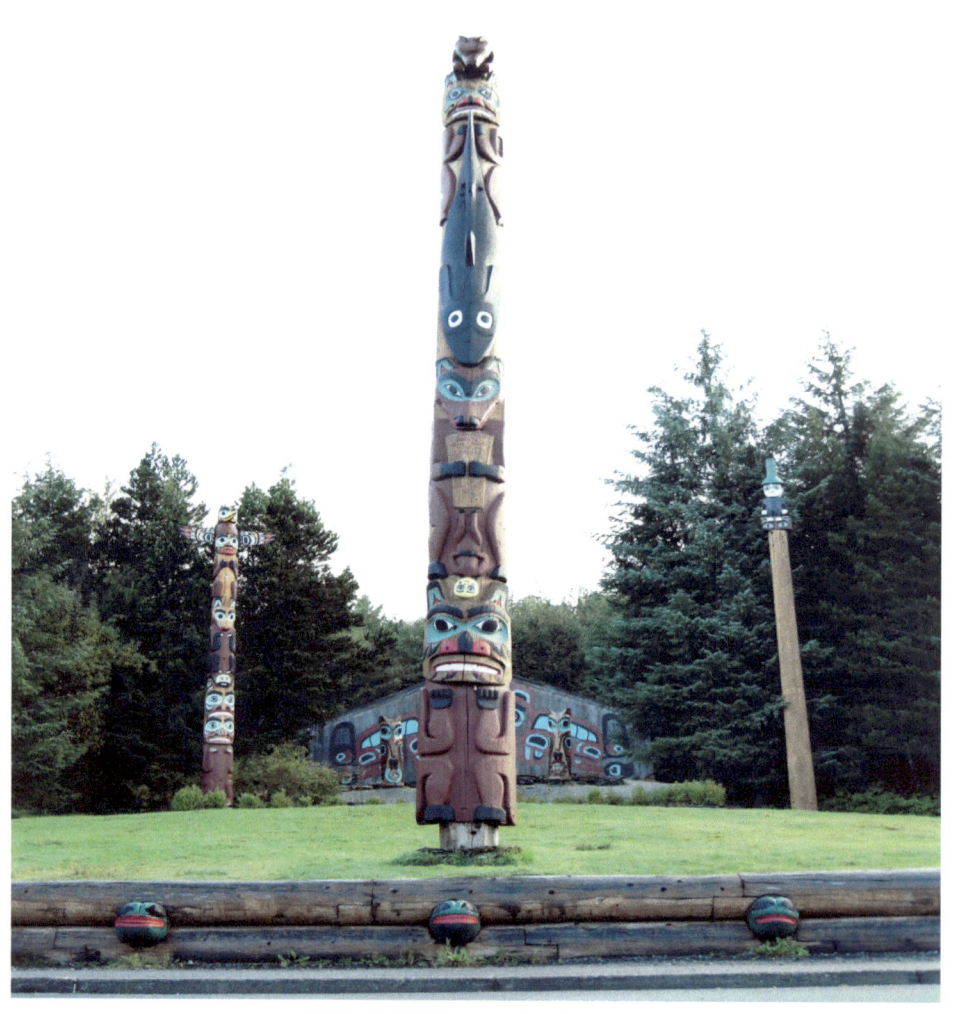

Chief Ebbits Pole (in center)

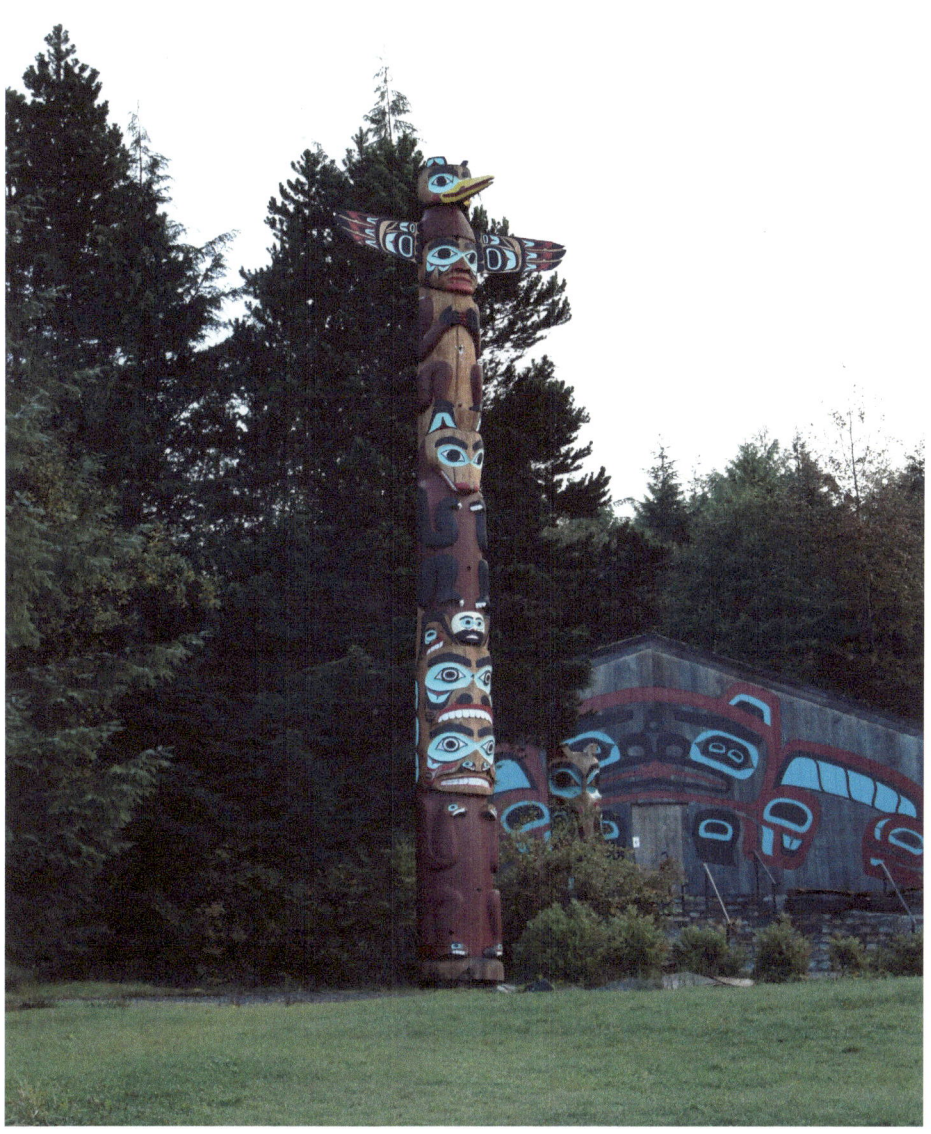

Eagle Pole

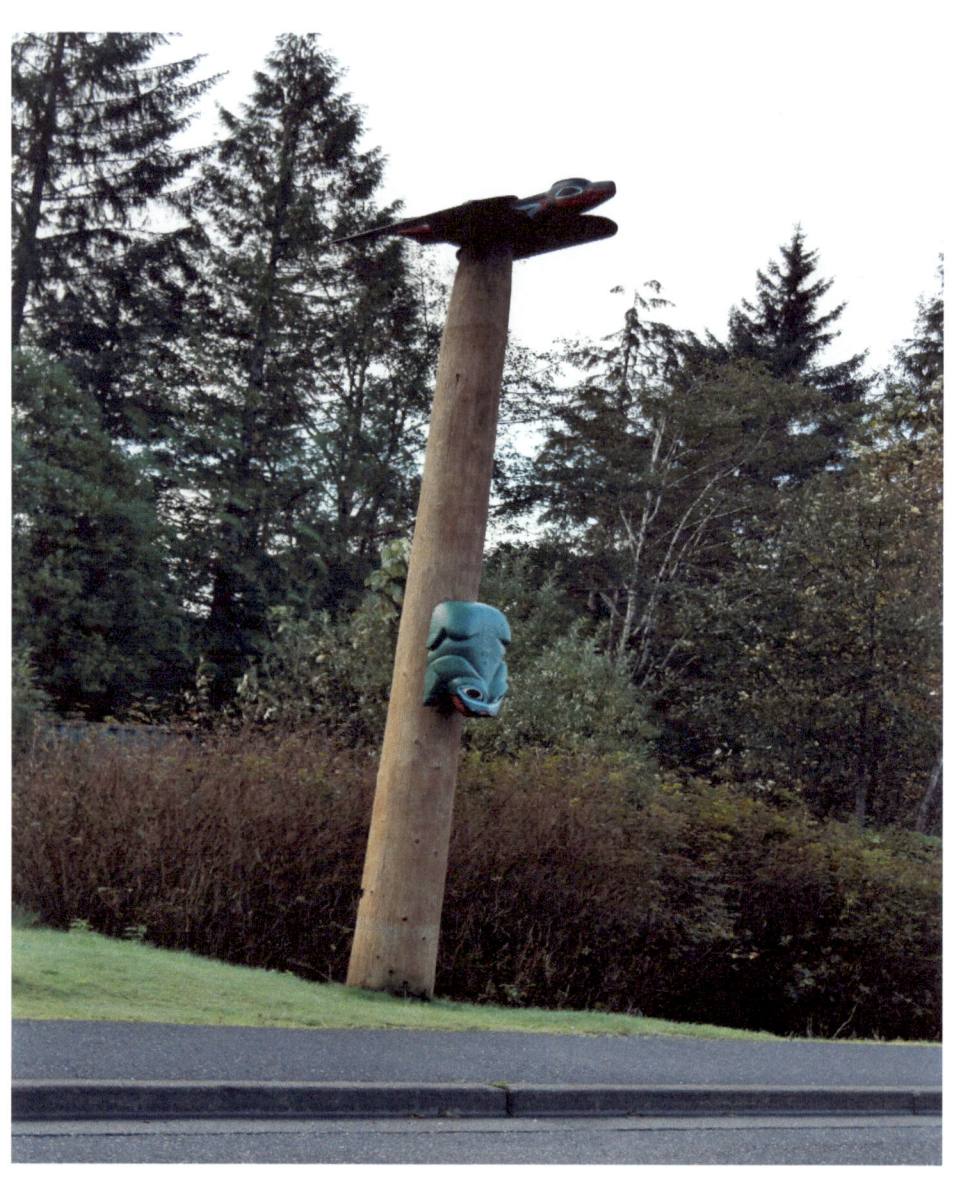

Raven and Frog Pole

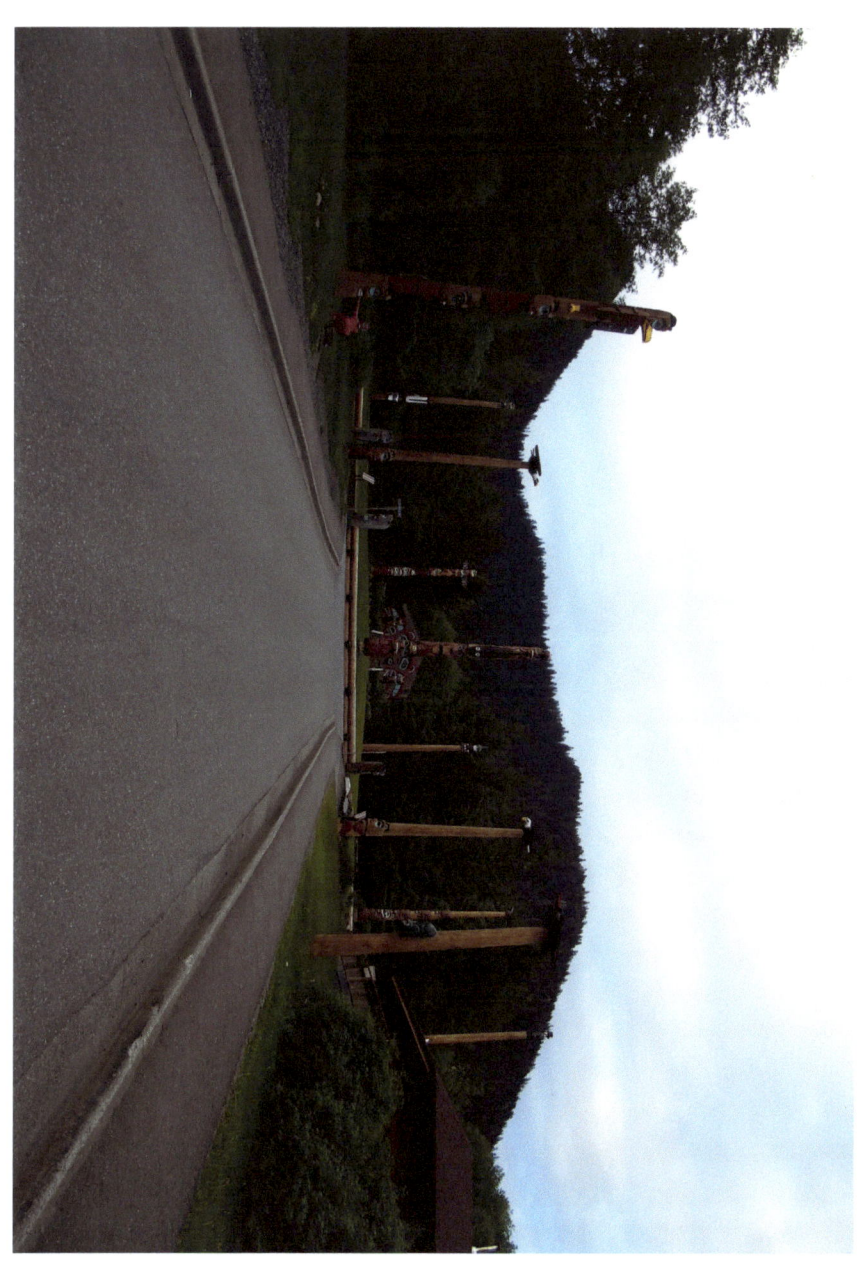

Saxman

Around Ketchikan

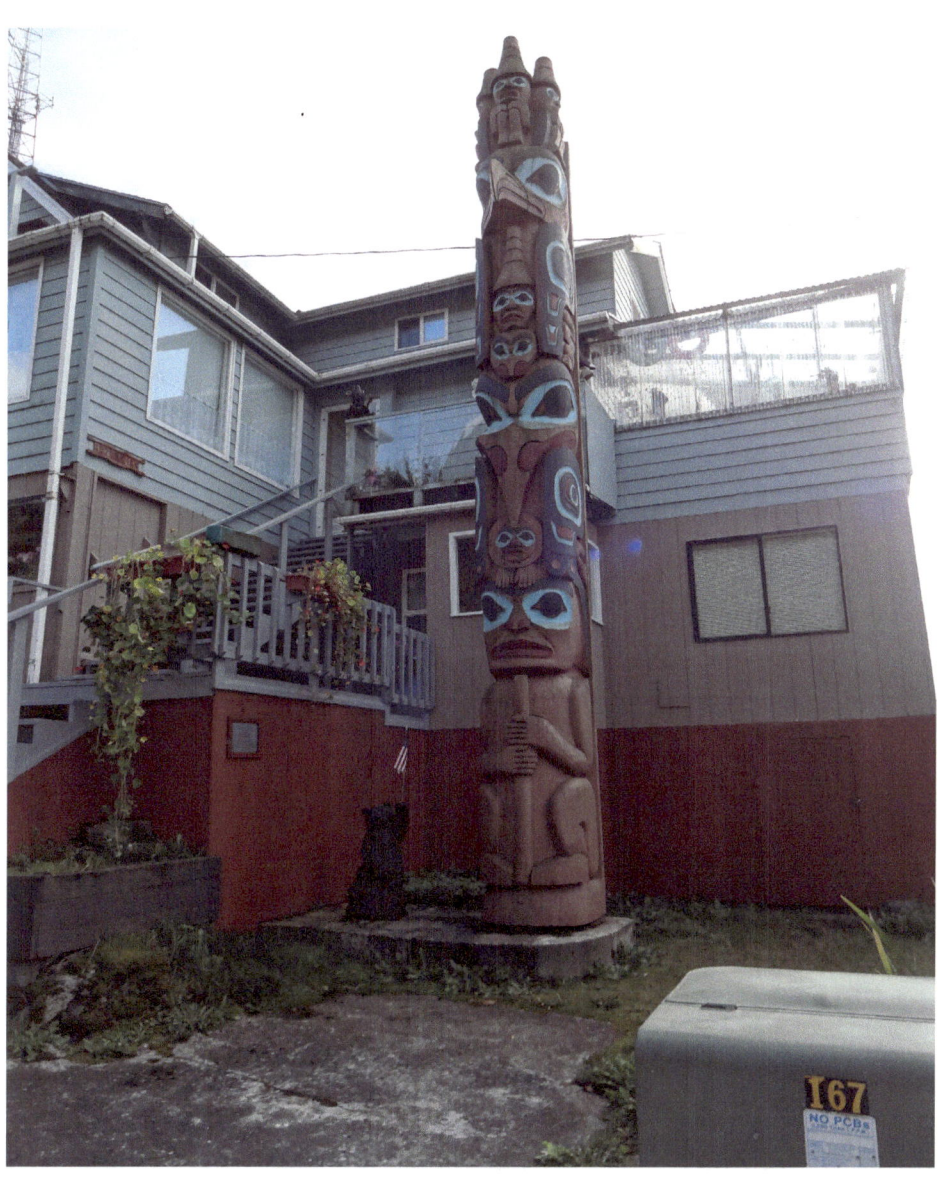

???

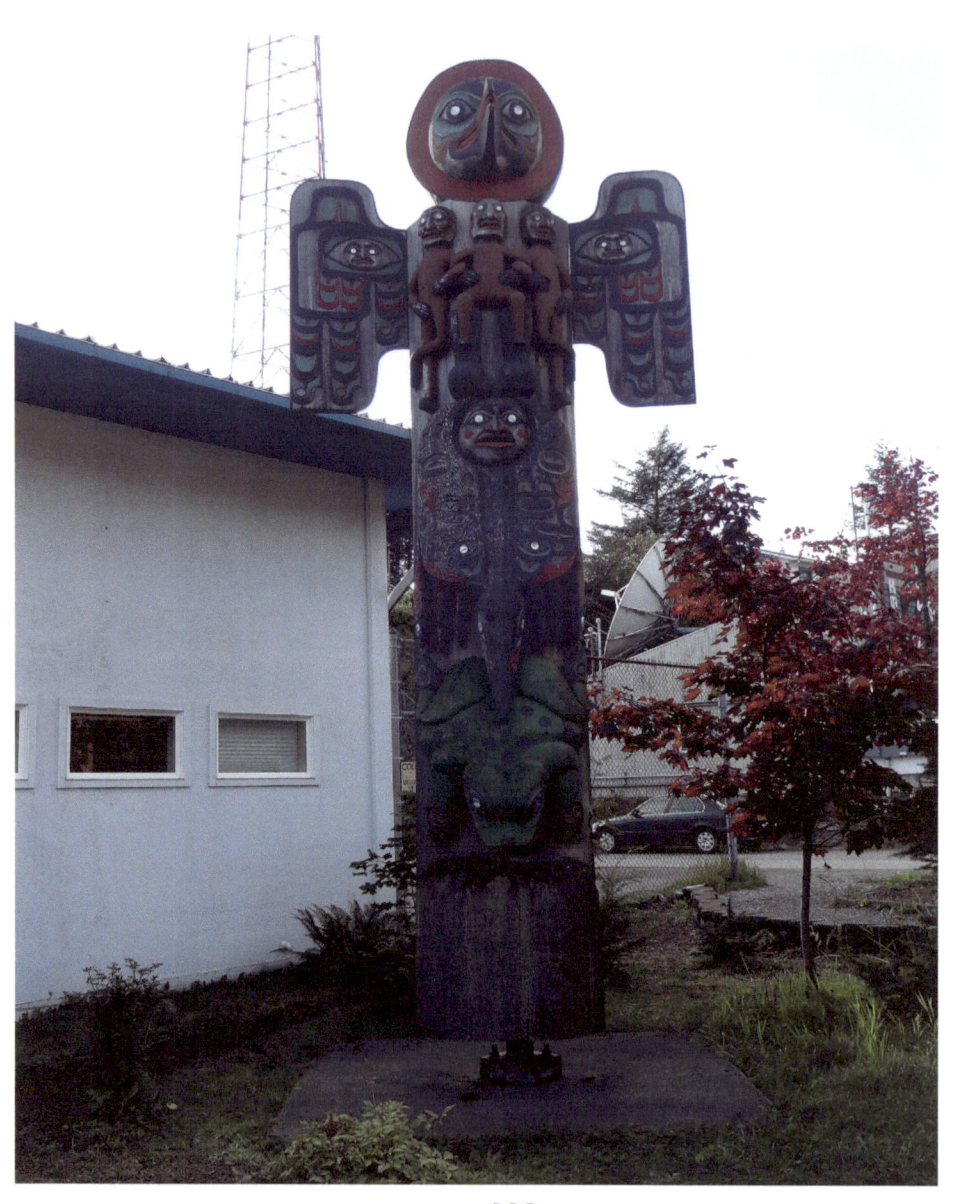
???

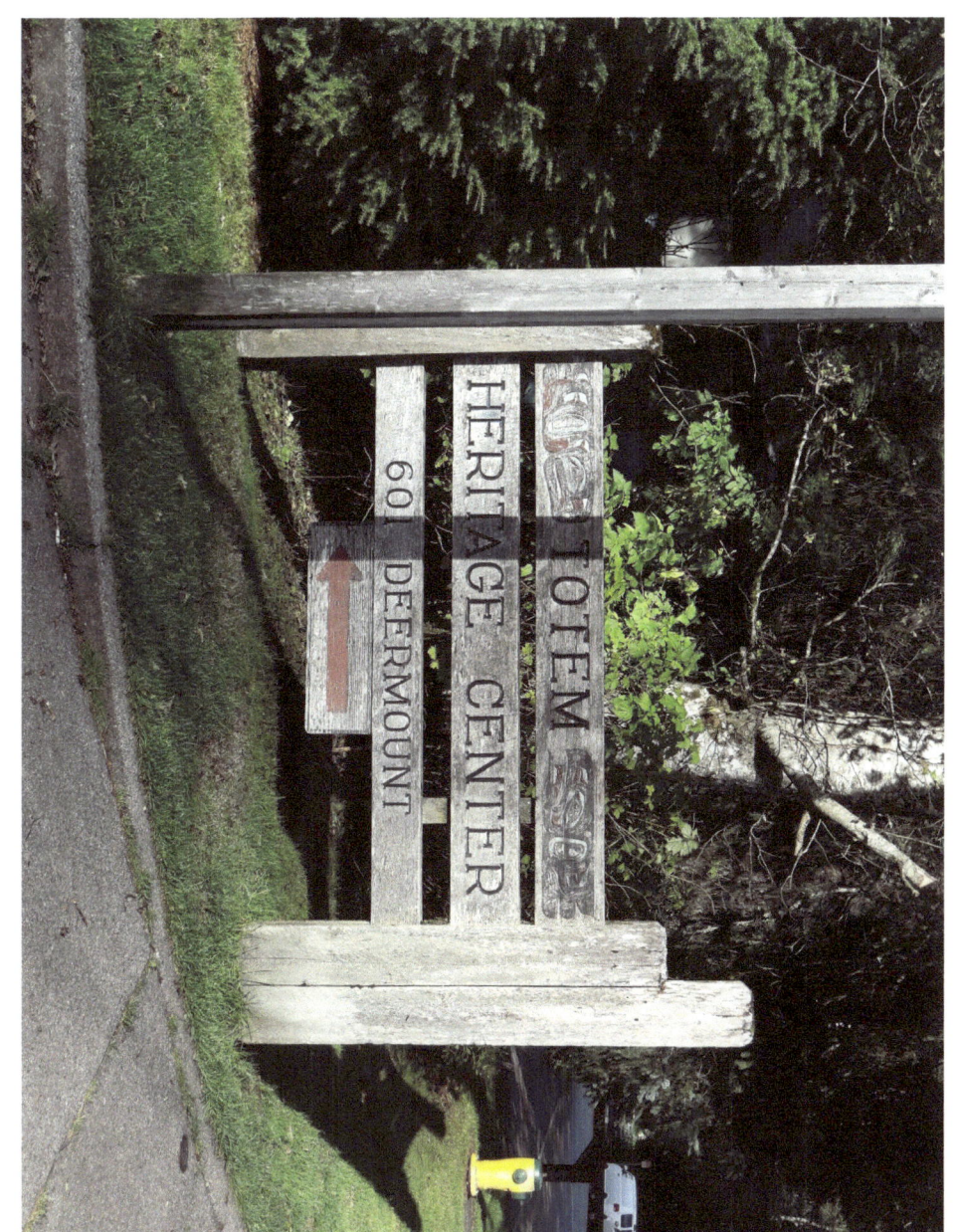

TOTEM HERITAGE CENTER

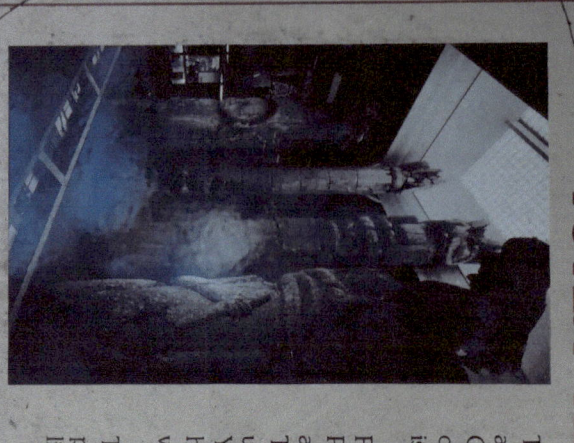

The Totem Heritage Center, a contemporary interpretation of a traditional Native community house, was built in 1976 by the City of Ketchikan to protect, preserve, and exhibit the only original totem pole collection in the United States. The collection is listed in the National Register of Historic Places.

From 1967 - 1970, the project "Alaska Totems: A Heritage in Peril", retrieved 33 poles, houseposts, and fragments from abandoned Tlingit and Haida villages surrounding Ketchikan. Totem poles flourished from mid-1700's to early 1900's and are unique to coastal areas from British Columbia, Canada to Yakutat, Alaska. Carved to honor deceased ancestors, record history, social events, and oral tradition, the poles were never worshipped as religious objects.

The Center teaches Northwest-Coast Indian art classes, and presents exhibits, demonstrations and tours emphasizing the living culture of the Haida, Tlingit, and Tsimshian Indians.

Visit Ketchikan's other totem poles, and the only National Landmark collection of old original totem poles at the Totem Heritage Center, 601 Deermount Street

City of Ketchikan
Museum Department
Photo: Hall Anderson Photography

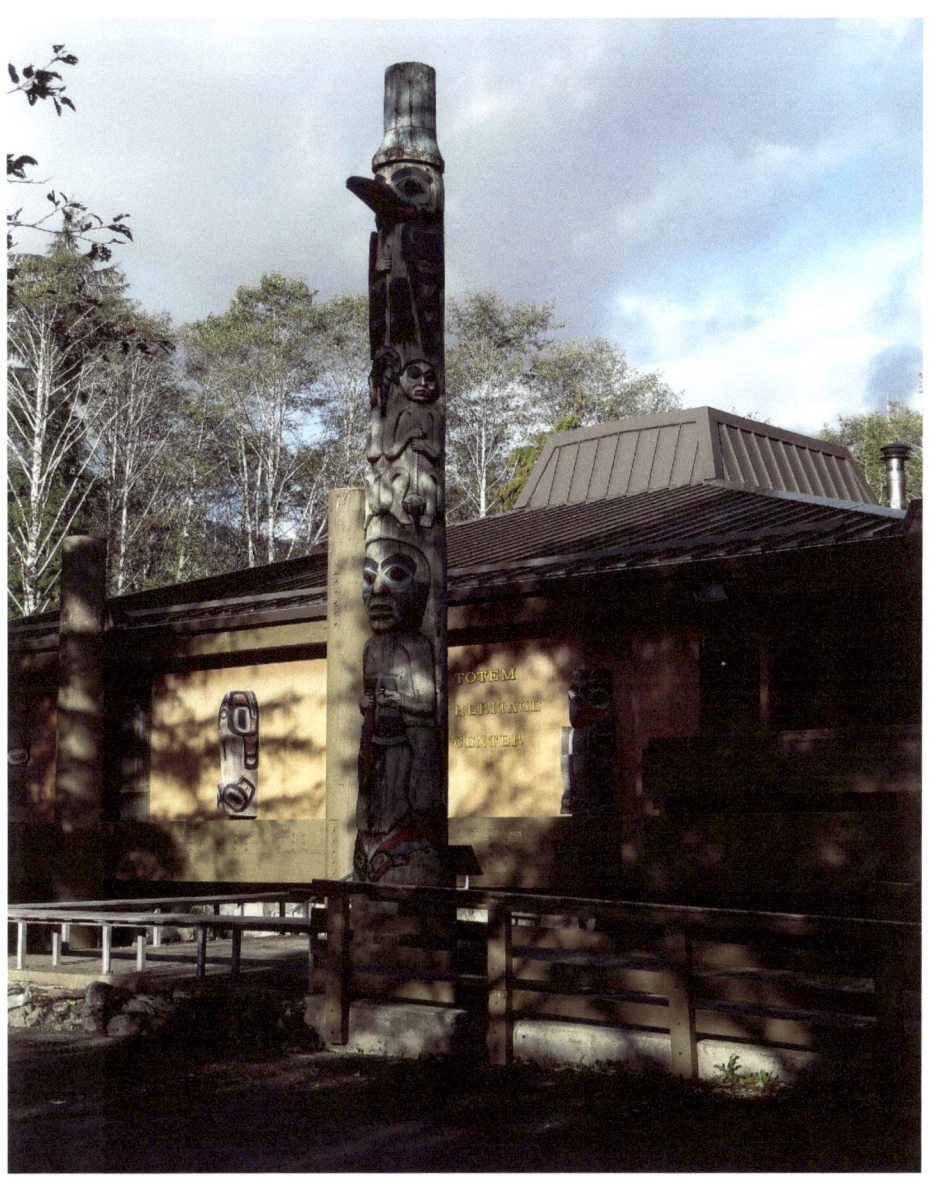

Totem Heritage Center

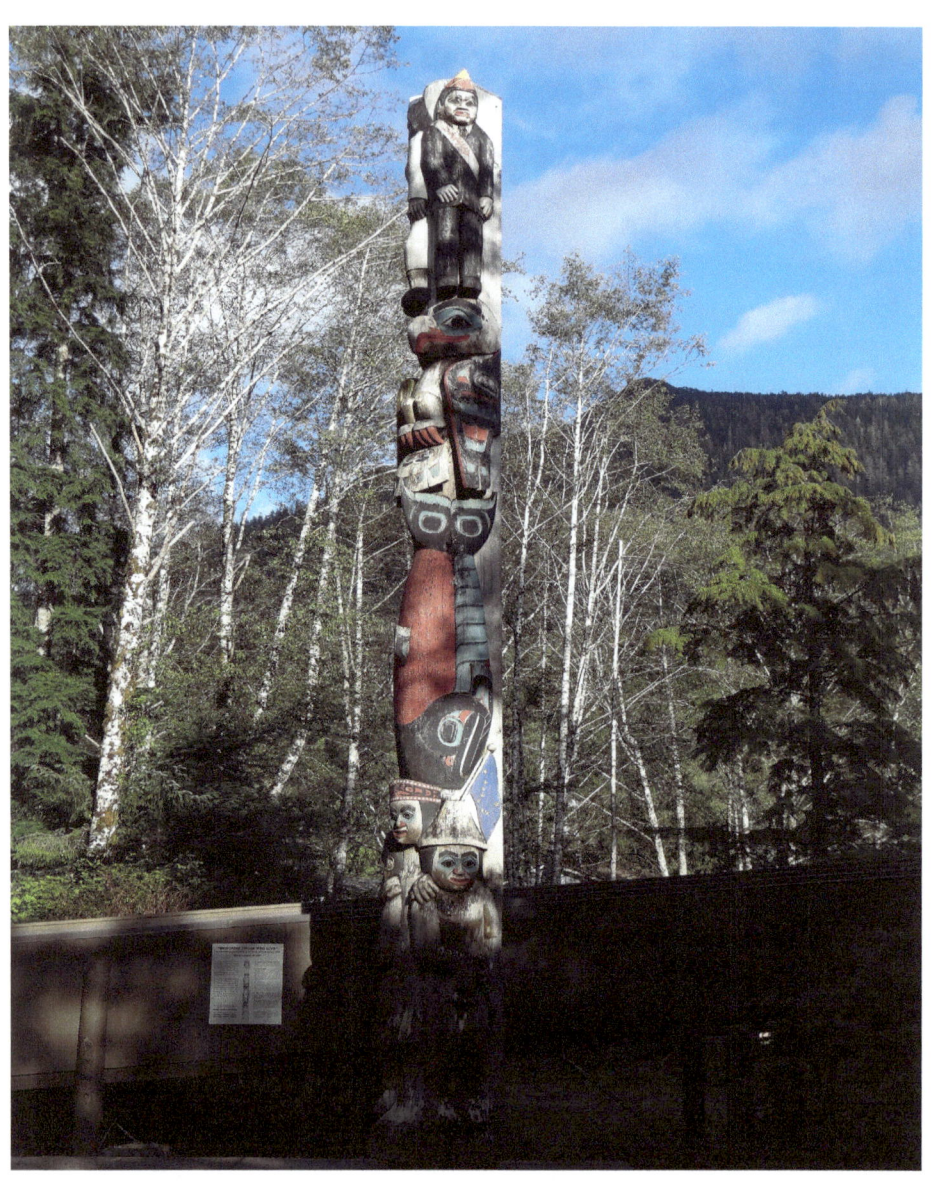

<u>Honoring those that give Pole – Totem Heritage Center</u>

"HONORING THOSE WHO GIVE"
Commemorating the Founding of the Totem Heritage Center, 1976

Raised on August 28, 1999

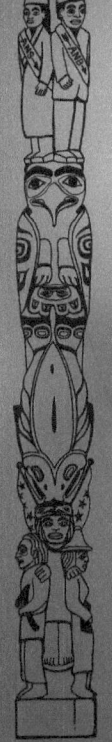

This totem pole was created by Nathan Jackson, Master Carver, who was born into the Sockeye Clan on the Raven side of the Chilkoot-Tlingit tribe. Apprentice carver Fred Trout assisted in the project.

The pole was commissioned by the City of Ketchikan to honor the individuals, organizations, and government entities that worked together to create the Totem Heritage Center and establish it as a leader in preserving traditional Northwest Coast Native arts.

❖

The project was made possible by a generous grant from the
Grand Circle Foundation
with additional support from the
Lila Wallace-Reader's Digest Community Folklife Program

In keeping with ancient tradition, the figures on this totem pole represent the elements of a story – in this case, the story of the founding of the Totem Heritage Center.

Two human figures at the top of the pole represent the Alaska Native Sisterhood and the Alaska Native Brotherhood. These organizations were instrumental in retrieving endangered totems from Native village sites and creating the Totem Heritage Center for the preservation of the poles. Both figures wear the Koogeinaa (sash) and hats that designate members of the ANS and ANB.

An eagle represents the federal government units that contributed to the project: the Smithsonian Institution and the Forest Service, which participated in the totem pole retrieval, and the Economic Development Administration, which provided funding for construction of the Totem heritage Center.

A king salmon represents the City of Ketchikan, which provided the site for the Totem Heritage Center and operates the facility as part of the City Museum Department.

Alaska State Flags represent the Alaska State Museum, which conceived and managed the totem retrieval project. The State holds the recovered poles in trust for the descendants of the original inhabitants of the Native villages from which the poles were removed.

Three human figures at the base of the pole represent students and instructors in the three areas of study in the Totem Heritage Center's Native arts curriculum: carving, ceremonial regalia, and weaving.

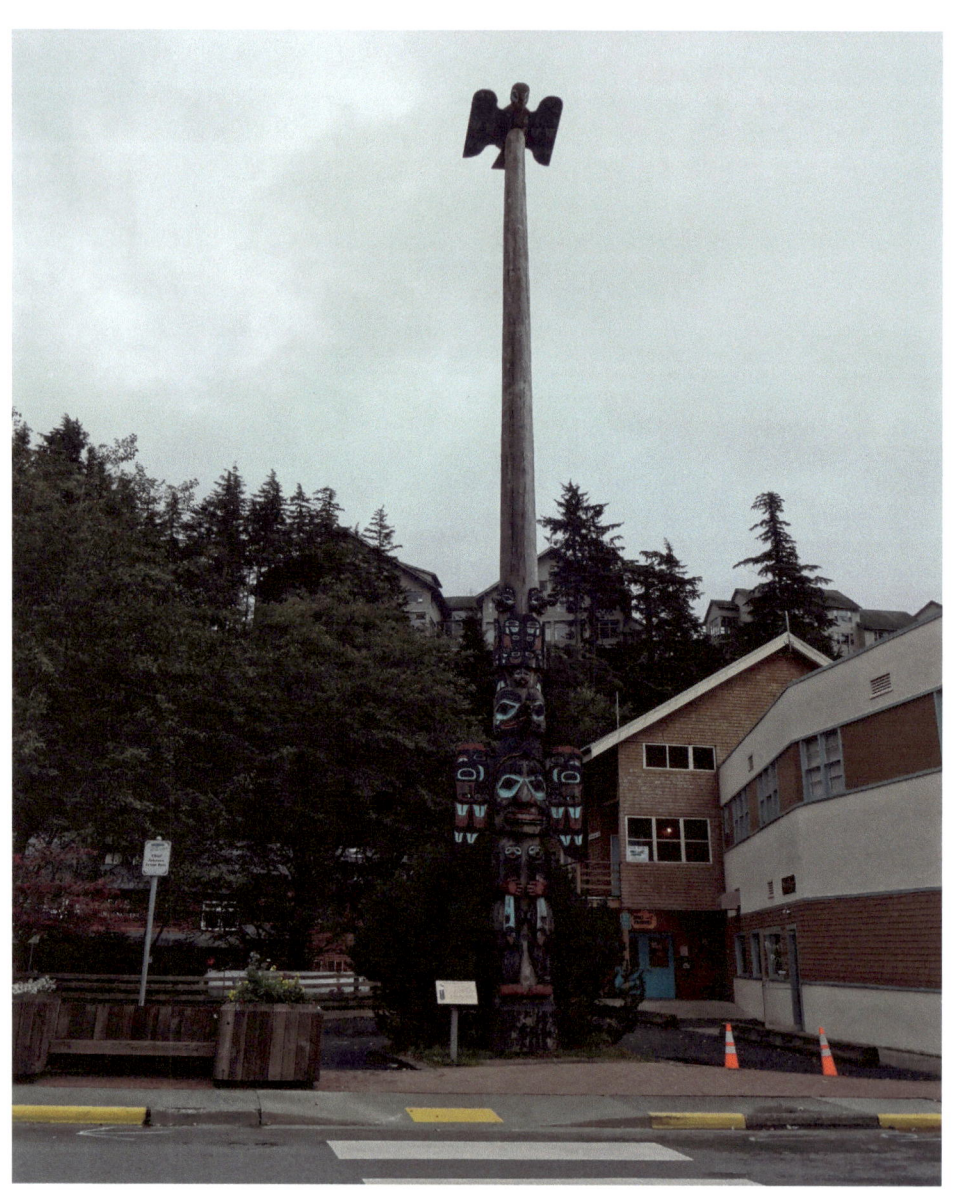

Chief Johnson Totem Pole

CHIEF JOHNSON TOTEM POLE

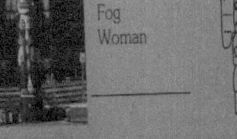

Kajuk
(fabled bird)

Undecorated
Space
symbol of
lofty habitat
and high
regard in
which the
crest is held

Raven's
Slaves

Raven

Fog
Woman

Totem poles are carved to honor deceased ancestors, record history, social events, and oral tradition. They were never worshipped as religious objects.

This totem, carved by Israel Shotridge and raised in 1989, is a replica of the Chief Johnson, or Kajuk, Totem Pole raised in this general location in 1901 for the Ganaxadi Tlingit of the Raven moiety of the Tanta Kwan (Tongass) group. The original memorial pole stood until 1982.

Except for Kajuk atop the pole, the figures symbolize a single story about Raven. Fog Woman is identified with the summer salmon run when fog lies at the mouth of streams. She produces all salmon and causes them to return to the creeks of their birth.

Visit Ketchikan's other totem poles, and the only National Landmark collection of old, original totem poles at the Totem Heritage Center, 601 Deermount Street.

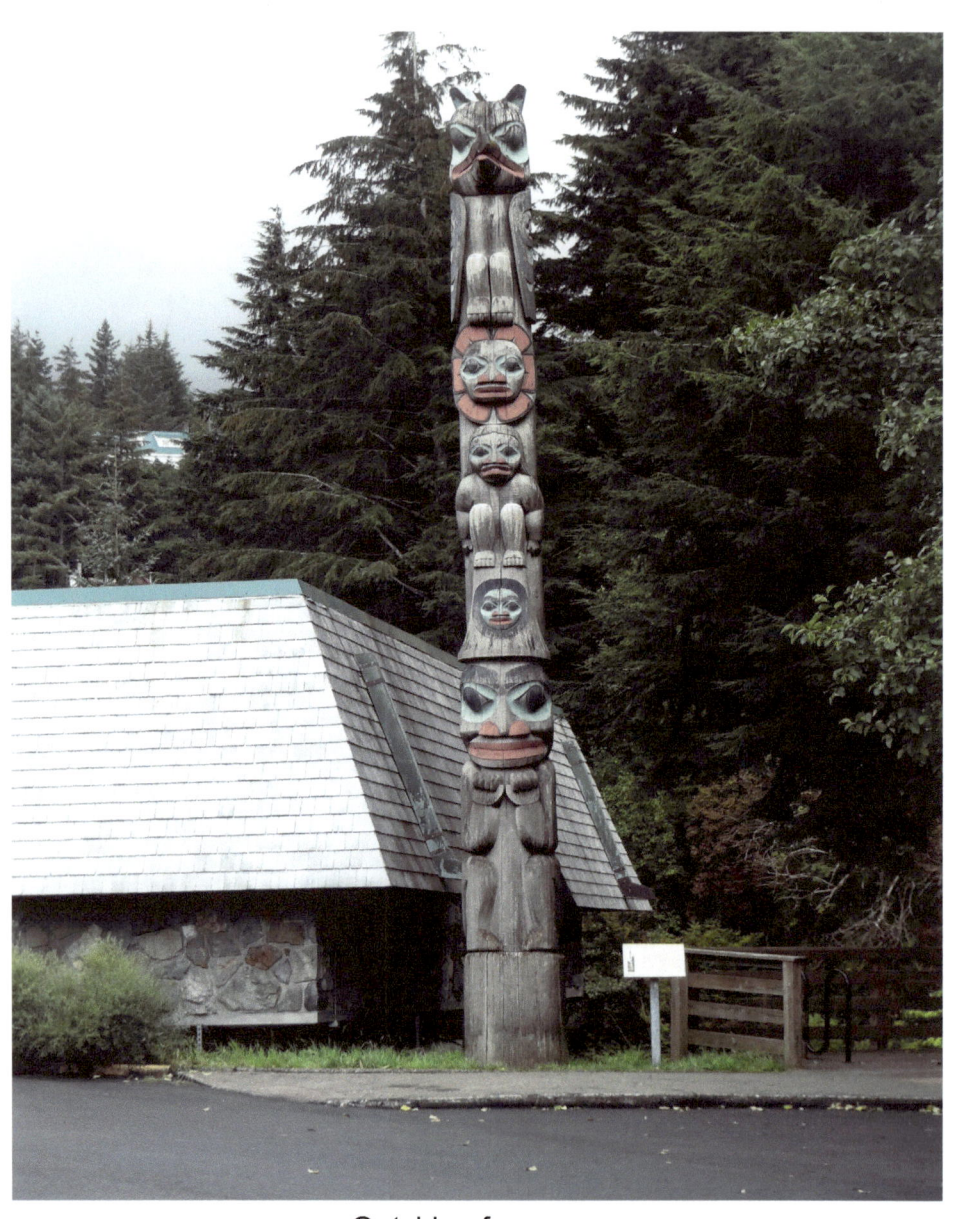

Outside of museum

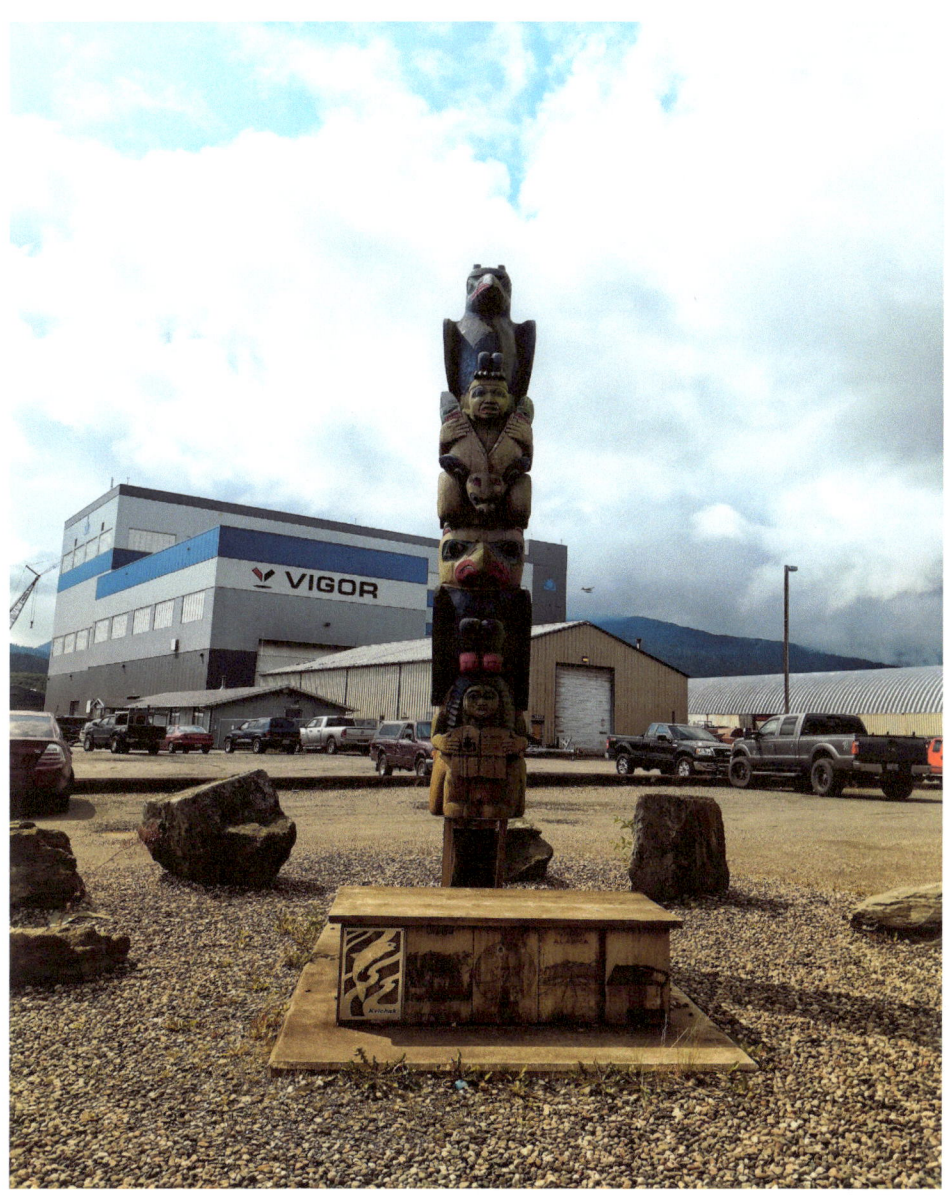

In front of Vigor

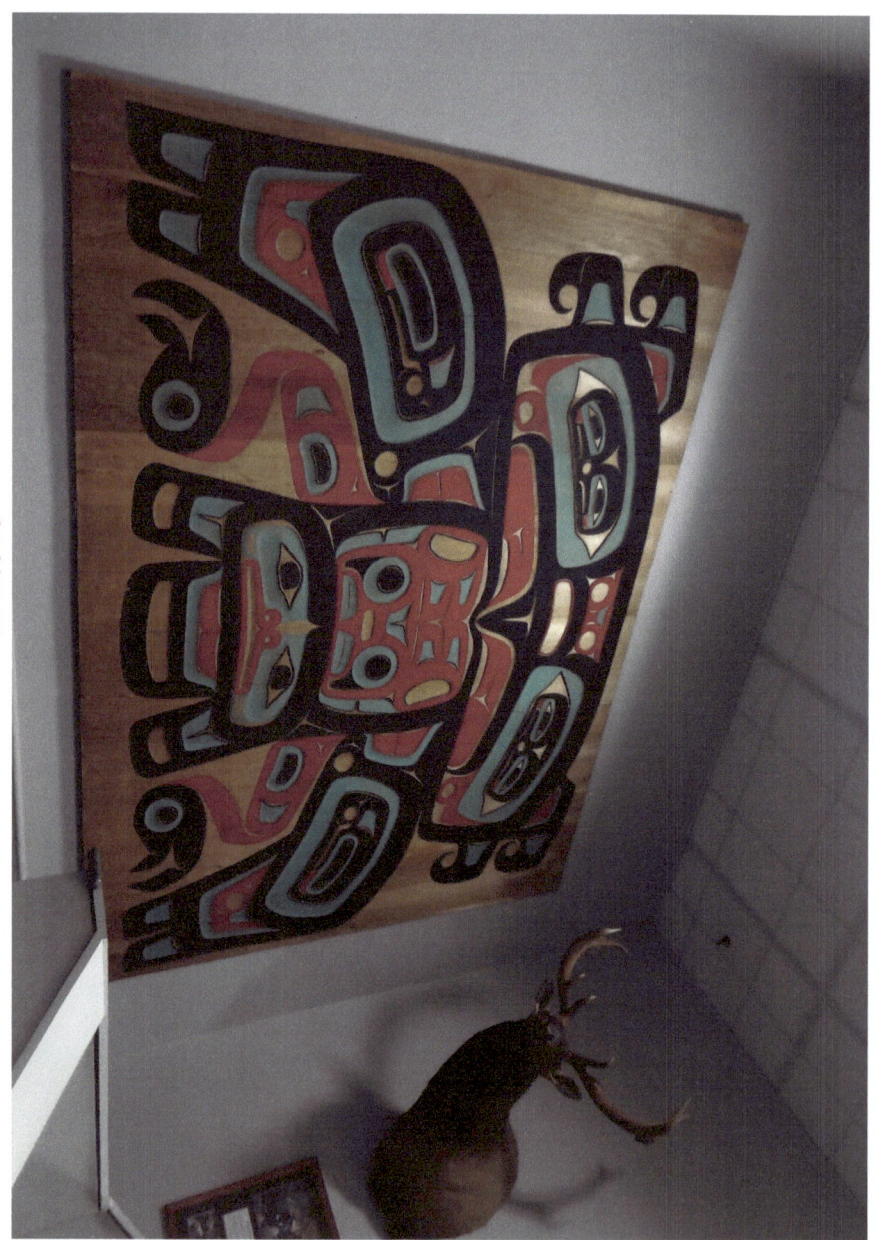

At Airport

Resources for info

- Pamphlet "Saxman Alaska – The Legend of the Totems"

- Pamphlet "Ketchikan Museums"

Online resources:

http://dnr.alaska.gov/parks/units/totembgh.htm

http://dnr.alaska.gov/parks/plans/totembight.pdf

https://en.wikipedia.org/wiki/Totem_pole

Pictures were taken using either a Sony A580 or a Sony A77ii, or a DJI Phantom 4 drone. No part of this book may be reproduced without the consent of the Author, unless it is for the purpose of a book review. You may email us at:
sp8s-studio@outlook.com

Sp8s Studio

Alaska and then some...

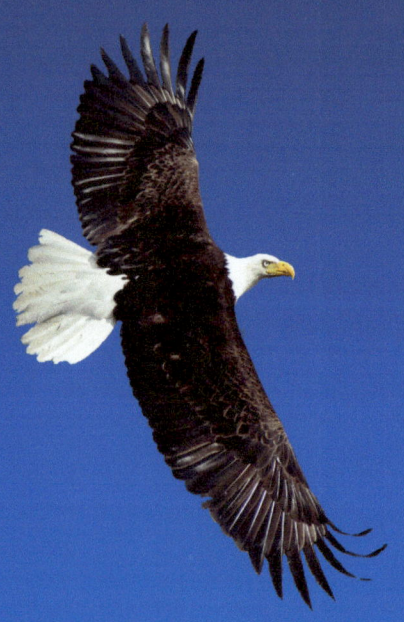

Pictures and Videos that will bring you back ...

www.Sp8sstudio.com

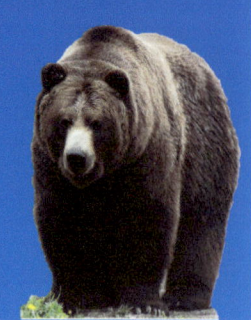